IT'S A MAN'S WORLD

Also by Judy Brown

1,349 Hilarious Jokes

Funny You Should Say That

Funniest Jokes from the World's Best Comedians

Jokes to Go

She's So Funny

IT'S A MAN'S WORLD

800 JOKES FROM THE GUY'S (WARPED) POINT OF VIEW

Judy Brown

BARNES
&NOBLE
BOOKS

NEW YORK

* ACKNOWLEDGMENTS *

First of all, I'd like to thank all the comedians who have such funny, pithy male stuff to say.

And then I'd like to thank my editor, Stuart Miller—such a guy's guy, that he was scared silly of my girly pink handbag. And thanks also to my assistant Andi Rhodes for transcribing manly man material when I was laughed out. Lastly, gracias to my favorite funny guy, my brother Bill, who knows how to keep a sister smiling: buy her jewelry.

* * *

Library of Congress Cataloging-in-Publishing Data
Available upon request

2005 Barnes & Noble Books

ISBN 0-7607-6829-3

Printed and bound in the United States of America

05 06 07 08 09 10 M 9 8 7 6 5 4 3 2 1

★ FOREWORD ★

It may no longer be a man's world exclusively, but for the sake of the little boy in all of you, I've constructed a joke version of The Little Rascals' He-Man Woman Haters Club: a book where male comedians promote masculine humor for guys who may feel nostalgic for those bygone days in which they seemed to get their way.

So g'wan, get comfortable, crack the spine of *It's a Man's World*, while you eat chili out of the can in your torn underwear, and scratch like a baseball player. Or, as you clutch the remote, even when the TV is off. Retreat with this book into your fortress of solitude, the bathroom. Feel free to act out any other stereotypically Y chromosome behavior: this book's for you.

Oh, by the way, there's an Easter egg hidden in this book: one joke, and one alone, was written by a woman comedian. There are clues, and the first man masculine enough to solve the riddle and sniff out the girl invader, gets a free copy of my joke book *She's So Funny: 1,815 of the Funniest Jokes from Women Comedians*.

Have fun,
Judy Brown

For info on comedy topics of all sorts, including my other joke books, comedy seminars, and publishing workshops:
e-mail: judy@judybrown.info
website: www.judybrown.info

I know a guy who had his nose broken in two places. He ought to stay out of those places.

— Henny Youngman

There was a 194-car crash in Los Angeles. Luckily the guy in the first car was still able to complete his cell phone call.

— Jay Leno

I think cops cause more accidents than they prevent. When you're driving and see a cop ahead, what do you do? Slam on the brakes and struggle to get your seatbelt on. Next to every accident you always see a police car. Coincidence? I think not.

— Rob O'Reilly

When I saw a car get sideswiped by a UPS truck, I had to leave a note. It said, "You have been hit by a UPS truck, but you were not in your car. This truck will return the same time tomorrow. If you are not in your car after a third accident, you can pick up your side-view mirror at the local UPS facility."

— Steve Hofstetter

* ACTIVISM *

I'd love to change the world, but I can't find a big enough diaper.

— Myq Kaplan

A lady came up to me on the street and pointed at my suede jacket. "Did you know a cow was murdered for that jacket?" she sneered. I replied in a psychotic tone, "I didn't know there were any witnesses. Now I'll have to kill you too."

— Jake Johannsen

My feeling is, we ran from animals for three million years, it's our time now. If a cow could eat you, it would. And it wouldn't care how comfortable your truck ride over was, either.

— Greg Proops

I volunteer with Habitat for Humanity. They build houses for people who otherwise couldn't afford them. I'm a do-it-yourselfer, and every once in awhile, it's nice to go and screw up someone else's house. I like to share my God-given inabilities.

— **Tony Deyo**

I got into an argument with an anti-war protester on the street the other day. And he said: "Alright, tough guy. Are *you* willing to go half way around the world and fight?" And I thought about it, and then I said, "Yes, I am." So in two weeks I'm going to Thailand to wrestle strippers.

— **Adam Gropman**

＊ ADULTERY ＊

It's a good marriage, but I think my wife has been fooling around. Because our parrot keeps saying, "Give it to me hard and fast before my husband Jonathan Katz comes home. And yes, I'd love a cracker."

— **Jonathan Katz**

I walked in the house, and my wife and my girlfriend were waiting for me. My girlfriend stood up and said, "I told her everything." I said to my wife, "You can't believe anything that woman says because last week she promised she wasn't gonna tell you nothin'."

— *Corey Holcomb*

I discovered my wife in bed with another man and I was crushed. So I said, "Get off of me, you two!"

— *Emo Philips*

According to the *British Journal of Psychiatry*, men cope with infidelity with denial. That's not true! That's a lie! I refuse to believe that!

— *Jay Leno*

Never tell. Not if you love your wife . . . in fact, if your lady walks in on you, deny it. Yeah. Just flat out: "I'm telling ya. This chick came downstairs with a sign around her neck, 'Lay on Top of Me, or I'll Die.'"

— *Lenny Bruce*

I will not cheat on my wife. Because I love my house.

— *Chas Elstner*

* ADVERTISING *

I saw a TV commercial that said, "Kiss your hemor-
rhoids goodbye." Not even if I could.

— *John Mendoza*

The basic beer ad: big-breasted babes in bikinis. Beer
won't get you babes. But if you drink enough, you
think they're babes, and if you drink more, you can
grow your own breasts.

— *Norman K.*

* AFFIRMATIVE ACTION *

How come the white male politicians who vote
against affirmative action are always so willing to
accept a handicap on the golf course?

— *Paul Krassner*

* AGING *

When you get older your body changes. I've noticed it myself. Now I groan louder after a meal than I do after an orgasm.

— Joel Warshaw

I know I'm getting older, I pulled my left shoulder out putting peanut butter on a bagel. It was chunky, though. I pulled out my right shoulder putting Ben-Gay on my left shoulder.

— Jeff Cesario

It used to be that my age and waist size were the same size. Unfortunately, they still are.

— Reno Goodale

I wake up in the morning, it takes me a half hour to find my glasses, just so I can look for my teeth, to tell my wife to find my hair.

— Richard Jeni

You know you're getting old, there are certain signs. I walked past a cemetery and two guys ran after me with shovels.

— Rodney Dangerfield

A guy says, "I'm so old that I forgot how old I am." An old woman says, "I'll tell you how old you are. Take off your clothes and bend over." The man does this. The woman says, "You're seventy-four." The man says, "How can you tell?" The woman says, "You told me yesterday."

— Henny Youngman

Some sad news, the world's oldest man has died in Japan at the age of a hundred and fourteen. What's the deal with this world's oldest title? It's like some kind of curse, have you noticed? As soon as you get it, like a year later, you're dead.

— Jay Leno

I'm so old that when I order a three-minute egg they make me pay up front.

— Henny Youngman

* ALCOHOL *

Is it bad when you refer to all alcohol as "Pain Go Bye-Bye Juice?"

— Patton Oswalt

Booze makes you loud. It's written on the label, "Alcohol percent by volume."

— Mark Lundholm

It's always interesting to see what receipts are in your pocket the morning after margaritas.

— Jason Love

One tequila, two tequila, three tequila, floor.

— George Carlin

Alcohol kills brain cells. We take the only organ in our body that won't grow back, and we kill it for fun.

— Cary Odes

If you enjoy your alcohol, remember this: if you put your old, rotten, used-up liver under your pillow, the Beer Fairy will leave you a keg.

— Paul F. Tomkins

My Dad was the town drunk. A lot of times that's not so bad, but New York City?

— Henny Youngman

* ANIMALS *

My wife works at an animal rescue place. So at home we now have a dog with two anuses, and half a dachshund.

— Jon Stewart

As part of a mass wedding ceremony in Thailand, "Guy," a chicken, married "Guk," a rooster. And, for the record, on their wedding night, the chicken came first.

— Jimmy Fallon

Size isn't everything. The whale is endangered, while the ant continues to do just fine.

— Bill Vaughan

The Discovery Channel had a fascinating show on the mating habits of hyenas. They said that the male hyena often will get angry at the female hyena while they are having sex. It doesn't help that the female hyena is laughing at you all the time.

— Jay Leno

I found a snake in my yard, and got a shovel and whacked the hell out of it. Then I didn't have cable for a week.

— Charlie Viracola

* APHRODISIACS *

An aphrodisiac is a drug two people take, and then both pretend it worked.

— *Strange de Jim*

* ARGUMENTS *

I got into an argument with my girlfriend inside a tent. A tent is not a good place for an argument. I tried to walk out on her and had to slam the flap.

— *Mitch Hedberg*

I don't know where my wife went to learn how to argue, but she really got good at it there.

— *John Heffron*

I got into a fight one time with a really big guy, and he said, "I'm going to mop the floor with your face." I said, "You'll be sorry." He said, "Oh yeah? Why?" I said, "Well, you won't be able to get into corners very well."

— *Emo Philips*

I got a gas grill, but it came unassembled. It looked like a car bomb. Every guy's been where I've been. You finish building it, it looks great, but there's a weird bag of important-looking stuff left over. I call my wife over, "Honey? Why don't you try the grill out first? I'll be in the basement with my welding hat on."

— *Tim Allen*

* ASSES *

Never comment on a woman's rear end. Never use the words "large" or "size" with "rear end." Never. Avoid the area altogether. Trust me.

— *Tim Allen*

* ASTROLOGY *

My wife's an earth sign. I'm a water sign. Together we make mud.

— Henny Youngman

* AUTOMOBILES *

My aunt, 30 years a feminist says, "A car is just an extension of your penis." Oh, I wish.

— Tim Allen

I'm having car problems. My *Check Engine* light came on today. But I couldn't check it, there was too much smoke. Then the *Game Over* light came on. I hadn't seen that one before.

— Dobie Maxwell

I've finally got a car that turns heads. Mostly because of the knocking, rattling, and backfiring.

— Reno Goodale

They recall a lot of cars. "We gotta get those cars back. We don't recall putting brakes in them."

— Evan Davis

Anybody abuse rental cars? The thing that bothers me is when you have to return one with a full tank of gas. You know what I do now? I just top it off with a garden hose.

— **Will Shriner**

According to some commercials, driving an SUV means you support terrorists. The answer is the hybrid gas-electric car, which only supports terrorists when going uphill.

— **Jon Stewart**

Los Angeles is now confiscating the cars of men who solicit prostitutes. The hardest part is asking your wife for a ride to work the next day.

— **Jay Leno**

Talking cars. Remember those? They'd tell you really stupid crap like, "*Your door is ajar.*" If a car is going to talk to me, I'd like it to be more informative. If I'm on a date with a girl, "*She's not wearing panties.*" Or, I'm just driving around and have a lot on my mind, "*Don't worry, the baby isn't yours.*"

— **Todd Larson**

The gas-station attendant looks at the car and says, "You got a flat tire." I said, "No, the other three just swelled up."

— **Bill Engvall**

BABIES

The hardest thing in the world is making a kid happy after he's been circumcised.

— **Damon Wayans**

Baby ca-ca is like Kryptonite to a father. Even the dog says, "You don't rub *his* face in it."

— **Robin Williams**

You have got to change those diapers every day. When it says "six to twelve pounds" on the side of the Pampers box, they're not lying. That is all those things will hold.

— **Jeff Foxworthy**

When my son was born I had this dream that one day he might grow up to be a Nobel Prize winner. But I also had another dream that he might grow up to say, "Do you want fries with that?"

— **Robin Williams**

Do infants enjoy infancy as much as adults enjoy adultery?

— **George Carlin**

I never loved anyone so much at first meeting. But let's make no mistake why these babies come here: to replace us. We'll see who's wearing the diapers when all this is over.

— **Jerry Seinfeld**

If you pull at babies too hard, they'll spew like a can of beer. I used to shake up my daughter and hand her to people I didn't like. "Hold her just a minute, would ya?"

— **Jeff Foxworthy**

* BANKING *

I had a hard time at the bank today. I tried to take out a loan and they pulled a real attitude with me. Apparently, they won't accept the voices in my head as references.

— **Steve Altman**

A bank is a place that will lend you money, if you can prove that you don't need it.

— Bob Hope

When someone's using an ATM, you want be about six feet back. People get edgy around that ATM. They got their money out, their eyes are darting around. The other place I wanna be six feet away is urinals. ATMs and urinals: whenever someone is taking something valuable out of their pants you want to give them as much room as possible.

— Jerry Seinfeld

I went to the bank and went over my savings. I found out I have all the money that I'll ever need. If I die tomorrow.

— Henny Youngman

* BARS *

I went to the bar to have a few drinks. The bartender asked me, "What'll you have?" I said, "Surprise me." He showed me a naked picture of my wife.

— Rodney Dangerfield

I was in a bar the other night, hopping from barstool to barstool, trying to get lucky. But there wasn't any gum under any of them.

— Emo Philips

I once said to a woman in a bar, "What's your name?" She said, "Don't even bother." I said, "Is that an Indian name, because I'd like to meet Hot to Trot. Is she here?"

— Garry Shandling

I went up to a girl in a bar once and asked her where she was from. I guess she wasn't interested, because she said, "Mars." So I asked, "You need a ride home?"

— Ray Romano

Two guys walk into a bar. You'd think one of them would have seen it.

— Daniel Lybra

In baseball, during the game, in the stands, there's kind of a picnic feeling; emotions may run high or low, but there's not too much unpleasantness. In football, in the stands, you can be sure that at least twenty-seven times you're capable of taking the life of a fellow human being.

— George Carlin

I was never an athletic kid. One year I played Little League baseball and my dad was the coach. Halfway through the season he traded me to another family.

— David Corrado

I used to steal second base, and feel guilty and go back.

— Woody Allen

Baseball is so associated with sex. "He's playing the field," "He scored," "He didn't get to first base." "I struck out." Why? "She wanted a diamond."

— Jerry Seinfeld

Another umpire was attacked by a fan. That's not fair. With their poor eyesight you know umpires can't pick suspects out of lineups.

— Jay Leno

* BASKETBALL *

My parents sent me to basketball fantasy camp. I got to sleep in the same bed with Patrick Ewing. Except I like a fan, and the noise kept him awake.

— *Adam Sandler*

You know the basketball game is decided when the white guys come in.

— *Jason Love*

Shaq has gotten so big his toes look like people. Ooh, he'll get mad at me for saying that. I'll just dress like a free throw, and he'll miss me.

— *D. L. Hughley*

* BATHROOMS *

A Turkish woman was arrested for keeping her husband locked in the bathroom naked for three years. Is that really the worst thing to do to a guy, lock them in the bathroom alone? You slide a pizza and a newspaper under the door, that's most guys' idea of a vacation. Do you know what the worst part was? Not only did the wife lock him in a bathroom for three years, but she wouldn't let him use the guest towels, either.

— *Jay Leno*

During the summer I like to go to the beach and make sand castles out of cement. And wait for kids to run by and try to kick them over.

— James Leemer

I went to the nude beach, but they didn't like me there. You're not supposed to wear anything, and I was wearing a video camera.

— Dan St. Paul

I bought a house on the beach. I thought it was a nude beach, but it turned out to be a giggle beach. When I appeared, everybody giggled.

— Adam Sandler

* BIRTH *

It was probably a coincidence, but right after I was born, mom and dad left town.

— Bob Hope

She's screaming like crazy . . . You have this myth you're sharing the birth experience. Unless you're circumcising yourself with a chain saw, I don't think so. Unless you're opening an umbrella up your ass, I don't think so!

— Robin Williams

My wife, God bless her, was in labor for 32 hours. And I was faithful to her the entire time.

— Jonathan Katz

I was born by cesarean section, but you can't really tell. Except that when I leave my house, I always go out the window.

— Steven Wright

I don't get no respect. When I was born, the doctor smacked my mother.

— Rodney Dangerfield

In the natural childbirth classes my wife and I took, the birthing process was represented by a hand puppet being pushed through a sock. So at the actual birth I was shocked to see all this blood. The thing I had prepared myself for was a lot of lint.

— Steve Skrovan

The doctor turned to me and asked, "Would you like to cut the cord?" And I said, "Isn't there anyone more qualified?"

— Bob Goldthwait

My friends want to show me films of their baby's birth. No, thank you. But I'll look at a video of the conception, if you've got one.

— Garry Shandling

* BIRTHDAYS *

I walked into a store and said, "It's my wife's birthday. I'd like to buy her a beautiful pen." The clerk winked at me and said, "A little surprise, heh?" I said, "Yes, she's expecting a Cadillac."

— Henny Youngman

My wife wanted a big party for our son's first birthday. I thought my idea was better, that we take him to the county fair, put him on a pony and have his picture taken. Then I'd take the picture home, and put it in a drawer. Eight or nine years from now when he finds the picture and comes to me to ask, "Dad, what was this?" I can say, "Son, that was your first birthday when I bought you a pony. One day I had to go out of town, and your Mom didn't take care of him and he died."

— **Jeff Jena**

For my birthday, my old man showed me a picture of a cake. I sat there all day trying to blow out the candles.

— **Rodney Dangerfield**

Why is it that with birthday cakes you can blow on them and spit on them and everyone rushes to get a piece?

— **Bobby Kelton**

On my sixteenth birthday my parents tried to surprise me with a car, but they missed.

— **Tom Cotter**

A bunch of friends threw a surprise party for me the other day . . . well, actually it was an intervention.

— **Steve Moris**

My childhood was rough. Once for my birthday, my old man gave me a bat. The first day I played with it, it flew away.

— Rodney Dangerfield

* BOXING *

Take boxing, the simplest, stupidest sport of all. It's almost as if these two guys are just desperate to compete with each other, but they couldn't think of a sport. So they said, "Why don't we just pound each other for forty-five minutes? Maybe someone will come watch that."

— Jerry Seinfeld

There's always one of my uncles who watches a boxing match with me and says, "Ten million dollars. For that kind of money, *I'd* fight him." As if someone is going to pay $200 a ticket to see a 57-year-old carpet salesman get hit in the face once and cry.

— Larry Miller

I love boxing. Where else do two grown men prance around in satin underwear fighting over a belt? The one who wins gets a purse. They do it in gloves. It's the accessory connection I love.

— John McGivern

Boxing gyms are still pretty much a man's domain, but now some women are stepping into the ring and onto the canvas. I don't get it. Doesn't it hurt? Damn straight it hurts. It's a man's place to pretend something doesn't hurt.

— Tim Allen

* BRAINS *

The average human uses less than ten percent of his brain and the average consumer buys high-tech electronic equipment and uses less than ten percent of the available features. Therefore, I define a genius as someone who can program a DVD player using the remote menu function.

— Dave Pavone

There is one thing I would break up over, and that is if she caught me with another woman. I wouldn't stand for that.

— **Steve Martin**

I just broke up with my girlfriend, because I caught her lying. Under another man.

— **Doug Benson**

I broke up with my girlfriend. She moved in with another guy, and I draw the line at that.

— **Garry Shandling**

I broke up with someone, and she said, "You'll never find anyone like me again." And I'm thinking, I hope not! If I don't want you, why would I want someone just like you? Does anybody end a bad relationship and say, "By the way, do you have a twin?"

— **Larry Miller**

I wasn't the easiest guy to live with, I had multiple personalities, but what bothered her was that none of them made any money.

— **Danny Liebert**

Refusal to accept reality does not change reality. My girlfriend broke up with me. I said, "I can't imagine you leaving me." She said, "Well, let me help. You stay here. I'm going to turn around. Then I'm going to start walking. To you, it'll seem like I'm getting smaller."

— **Basil White**

A woman broke up with me, and sent me pictures of her and her new boyfriend in bed together. Solution? I sent them to her dad.

— **Christopher Case**

I asked my ex-girlfriend, "Do you think we'll get back together?" She said, "I think the chances are better of me putting Super Unleaded into a rented car."

— **David Spade**

* BREAST-FEEDING *

I can't get past the fact that food is coming out of my wife's breasts. What was once essentially an entertainment center has now become a juice bar.

— **Paul Reiser**

It ain't easy being me, my mother breast-fed me through a straw.

— **Rodney Dangerfield**

My mother breast-fed me with powdered milk. It was my first real do-it-yourself project.

— **Buzz Nutley**

My mother never breast-fed me. She told me that she only liked me as a friend.

— **Rodney Dangerfield**

Those stupid laws that say the person being breast-fed in public has to be a baby.

— **Norm Macdonald**

A child is too old to breast-feed when he can unhook mommy's bra with one hand.

— **Anthony Clark**

Fake breasts, women always say, "You know they're not real, don't you? She bought them." I don't care if they're real. I want to buy some, too. For the house, put them in different rooms. And on the dashboard of the car, for when I'm driving.

— **Arsenio Hall**

* CAMPING *

Camping: that's what I call getting drunk outside.

— Dave Attell

* CANCER *

A study in Italy showed that people who eat a lot of pizza are less likely to get colon cancer. And another study says masturbation reduces risk of prostate cancer. It's what I've always said: diet and exercise.

— Jay Leno

* CANNIBALS *

Cannibals love Domino's Pizza. Not for the pizza, but for the delivery guy.

— Shang

* CARDS *

Card-playing can be expensive, but so can any game where you begin by holding hands.

— Henny Youngman

I was once asked to play Strip Poker, but I'm more comfortable with Strip Solitaire.

— Rob O'Reilly

I stayed up one night playing poker with tarot cards. I got a full house and four people died.

— Steven Wright

* CATS *

Cats are smarter than dogs. You can't get eight cats to pull a sled through snow.

— Jeff Valdez

One thing you can say about cats. They don't have to worry about kissing each other's asses; they can do that for themselves.

— Dwight

My wife's cats have been neutered and declawed, so they're like pillows that eat.

— Larry Reeb

I found our cat the other day. I would have found him a week ago, but we've got a grass bag on the lawn mower.

— Emo Philips

Construction workers rescued a cat completely encased in asphalt. The cat said the last thing it remembered was sharing a bag of catnip with two strippers.

— Craig Kilborn

People do crazy things when bored. I'm sitting at home with nothing to do, looking at the cats and think, "I'll teach the cats to wrestle." You should never teach cats to wrestle, but if you do, here's how: Get two cats. Take cat number one, and rub catnip all over him. Put him next to cat number two. The rest just sort of happens.

— Basil White

* CHEATING *

My girlfriend found out I was messing around with this other chick. So she called my wife.

— *Corey Holcomb*

A woman won't dump a man until she's found someone to replace him. In a woman's mind, if you cheat on her, it's because you're a jerk. But if she cheats on you, it's because you're a jerk.

— *Jeff Shaw*

* CHILDHOOD *

Once when I was lost I asked a policeman to help me find my parents. I asked him, "Do you think we'll ever find them?" He said, "I don't know, kid. There are so many places they can hide."

— *Rodney Dangerfield*

I'm nostalgic. I miss childhood. I miss first grade. I miss thinking girls are gross. Do you know how much money I could save if I still thought girls were gross?

— *Patrick Keane*

When I was a kid we had a quicksand box. I was an only child, eventually.

— Steven Wright

I was an only child growing up. I used to have to play with myself a lot. As a matter of fact, I still do.

— Erik Mackenroth

We were poor. If I wasn't a boy, I wouldn't have had nothing to play with.

— Redd Foxx

I don't get no respect. When I played in the sandbox, the cat kept covering me up.

— Rodney Dangerfield

I grew up hearing such stupid things. My mother would say, "That's the last time I'm gonna tell you to take out the garbage." Well, thank God.

— George Wallace

I was so nerdy as a kid, the only thing that would have made beating me more attractive is if I'd been filled with candy.

— Larry Getlen

How can any child resist the tooth fairy? That single shining example of selfless generosity in this slimy vale of greed. When I was broke, I pulled out my brother's teeth. Naturally, it was too good to last. Just one more nonrenewable resource on a diminishing planet.

— A. Whitney Brown

* CHRISTMAS *

The Supreme Court has ruled they cannot have a Nativity scene in Washington, D.C. This wasn't for any religious reasons. They couldn't find three wise men and a virgin.

— Jay Leno

Santa is very jolly because he knows where all the bad girls live.

— Dennis Miller

The day after Christmas, when we all have two more ugly sweaters.

— Craig Kilborn

Last Christmas, I got no respect. In my stocking I got an Odor-Eater.

— Rodney Dangerfield

The best stocking stuffer is a human leg.

— Norm Macdonald

For the holidays here in Los Angeles, women are getting snow-globe breast implants. When they jiggle it looks like it's snowing.

— Jay Leno

* CLICHES *

If you can't beat them, arrange to have them beaten.

— George Carlin

You are what you eat. Which makes me cheap, quick, and easy.

— Dave Thomas

Do unto others, then run.

— Benny Hill

I always wanted to be the last guy on earth, just to see if all those women were lying to me.

— Ronnie Shakes

The grass is always greener when someone else mows it.

— Jason Love

If I was stranded on a desert island and could only have one book, I would choose the one with the softest pages.

— Vinny Badabing

Life's a bitch. Then you marry one.

— Steve Carell

Life isn't like a box of chocolates, it's like a jar of jalapenos: you never know what's going to burn your ass.

— Paul Rodriguez

I was high on life, but eventually I built up a tolerance.

— Arj Barker

My granddad used to say, "If everybody liked the same thing, they'd all be after your grandma."

— Gary Muledeer

They say when you die there's a light at the end of the tunnel. When my father dies, he'll see the light, make his way toward it, and then flip it off to save electricity.

— Harland Williams

Just remember: it's lonely at the top, when there's no one on the bottom.

— Rodney Dangerfield

Love is the answer, but while you're waiting for the answer, sex raises some pretty good questions.

— Woody Allen

Love is blind. I guess that's why it proceeds by the sense of touch.

— Morey Amsterdam

If money can't buy happiness, then I guess I'll have to rent it.

— Weird Al Yankovic

Always look out for number one and be careful not to step in number two.

— **Rodney Dangerfield**

My father wore the pants in the family — at least, after the court order.

— **Vernon Chapman**

I've upped my standards. Now, up yours.

— **Pat Paulsen**

I'm a dreamer, but every time I reach for the stars my underpants get stuck in my butt.

— **Danny Liebert**

If at first you don't succeed, stay away from skydiving.

— **Milton Berle**

You can get more with a kind word and a gun, than you can with a kind word alone.

— **Johnny Carson**

Hard work pays off in the end, but laziness pays off now.

— **Al Lubel**

It's a small world, but I wouldn't want to paint it.

— **Steven Wright**

* CLONING *

Now that we can clone humans they've removed
the one pleasurable thing about having a child.

— David Letterman

* CLOTHING *

They should put expiration dates on clothing so we
men will know when they go out of style.

— Garry Shandling

A woman should dress to attract attention. To
attract the most attention, a woman should be
either nude, or wearing something as expensive as
getting her nude is going to be.

— P.J. O'Rourke

They say you can compare a man's shoe size to his manhood. So that's why I keep my skis on everywhere I go.

— Garry Shandling

The idea behind the tuxedo is the woman's point of view that men are all the same, so we might as well dress that way. That's why a wedding is like the joining together of a beautiful, glowing bride — and some guy. The tuxedo is a wedding safety device. In case the groom chickens out, everybody just takes one step over, and she marries the next guy.

— Jerry Seinfeld

* COFFEE *

I'm on decaf now. What I miss most is the road rage.

— David Letterman

There is now a Starbucks in my pants.

— George Carlin

* COLLEGE *

College: a fountain of knowledge where all go to drink.

— **Henny Youngman**

I went to college: majored in philosophy. My father said, "Why don't you minor in communications so you can wonder out loud?"

— **Mike Dugan**

The student loan director from my bank called. He said, "You've missed 17 payments, and the university never received the $17,000. We'd like to know what happened to the money." I said, "Mr. Jones, I'll give it to you straight. I gave the money to my friend Slick, and he built a nuclear weapon with it. And I'd appreciate it if you'd never call again."

— **Steven Wright**

I took biology two years in a row just to eat the specimens.

— Pat Paulsen

I was in the ROTC program. I remember once I was walking through campus and my instructor grabs me, and he's a real big guy, and yells, "It's been six weeks since I've seen you in camouflage class!" I said, "I'm getting good."

— Emo Philips

College is where I realized that God didn't need seven days to create the earth. He could party for six days, and pull an all-nighter.

— Tommy Koenig

Why do they say, "Give it the old college try?" Based on our experience, "the old college try" would consist of sleeping in for four years and not giving a damn.

— Lee Curtis & Jon Berahya

I had the worst study habits in the history of college, until I found out what I was doing wrong: highlighting with black Magic Marker.

— Jeff Altman

Comedy is when you accidentally fall off a cliff and die. Tragedy is when I have a hangnail.

— Mel Brooks

Women claim that what they look for in a man is a sense of humor, but I don't believe it. Who do you want removing your bra: Russell Crowe or the Three Stooges?

— Bruce Smirnoff

COMPUTERS

I just bought a computer. Fifteen-hundred bucks, with extra memory. Then I find out that for an extra $10, you can get one that holds a grudge.

— Jonathan Katz

I shop at a computer store called, "Your Crap is Already Obsolete."

— Jeff Cesario

They say that computers can't think, but I have one that does. It thinks it's broken.

— Gene Perret

CONCEPTION

I'd like to thank everyone who helped my parents conceive me. Grandma who babysat, Paul Masson for making chablis cheap enough for my Pops to buy three bottles, the Oldsmobile Cutlass Supreme for the roomy backseat which gave Pops the traction he needed to get into his love groove, and the pharmacist for supplying the defective prophylactic.

— Adam Sandler

* CONGRESS *

You can lead a man to Congress, but you can't make him think.

— Milton Berle

The Senate decided they will be smoke-free. They ordained that all public areas in the Senate are now smoke-free. However, the Senators themselves will still be allowed to blow smoke up each other's asses.

— Bill Maher

The reason there are two senators for each state is so that one can be the designated driver.

— Jay Leno

* CONTRACEPTION *

Contraceptives should be used on every conceivable occasion.

— Spike Milligan

Australian scientists say contraception is thousands of years old, and the first contraceptive was the jaw bone from a yak. The woman would hit the guy over the head with it.

— Jay Leno

I was insecure about sex. I've grown more secure. I used to use the amateur phylactics, and I only use the prophylactics now.

— Steve Martin

I wear two condoms all the time. Then when I make love, I take one off, and I feel like a wild man.

— Dennis Miller

They have ribbed condoms now that come with barbeque sauce.

— Jay London

Recently someone asked if I minded wearing a condom. Au contraire, I prefer them. There's no difference in the sensation, unless you count the total lack of any.

— Richard Jeni

I don't understand why some guys get self-conscious when they buy condoms. I don't get embarrassed when I buy condoms; I get embarrassed when I throw them out after they expire.

— Jack Archey

Condoms aren't completely safe. A friend of mine was wearing one and got hit by a bus.

— Bob Rubin

I opened my stuffed dresser drawer, and a box of condoms fell out of the back, and landed at the bottom of the dresser. And I thought, "This is my sex life: it's gotten so bad, my condoms are committing suicide." And the worst part is, they left a note. "Dear Larry: No one should ever be made to feel this useless for this long. Yours in misery, the Trojan Variety Pack."

— Larry Getlen

According to a new survey, fifty-six percent of women carry condoms. The other forty-four percent are carrying babies.

— Jay Leno

I was involved in an extremely good example of oral contraception two weeks ago. I asked a girl to go to bed with me, and she said "No."

— Woody Allen

A study says taking birth control pills makes a woman's voice more pleasant. Of course. "Yes" is always more pleasant than "no."

— Jay Leno

A birth control pill for men, that's fair. It makes more sense to take the bullets out of the gun, than to wear a bulletproof vest.

— Greg Travis

* COOKING *

Bachelor cooking is a matter of attitude. If you think of it as setting fire to things and making a mess, it's fun. It's not as much fun if you think of it as dinner. Nomenclature is an important part of bachelor cooking. If you call it "Italian cheese toast," it's not disgusting to have warmed-over pizza for breakfast.

— P.J. O'Rourke

* CRIME *

I used to get beaten up by these green berets in my neighborhood. Some people call them Girl Scouts.

— Tom Cotter

In France a woman shot her husband dead because of his flatulence. And now she gets the gas chamber.

— Jay Leno

A woman escaped death when a bullet shot by her jealous husband lodged in her breast implant. And I almost lost a thumb.

— Craig Kilborn

Some guy broke into our house last week. He didn't even take the TV. He just took the remote control. Now he drives by and changes channels on us.

— Brian Kiley

A woman cut off her husband's penis while he was sleeping after she got a phone call from another woman. The worst part: the other woman had the wrong number.

— Conan O'Brien

In Berlin a laundromat was raided because it was a front for a brothel. You know what tipped police off? Men doing laundry.

— Jay Leno

* DANCING *

I have heard women say they can judge how a guy will be in bed from how he dances. I hope that's not true. Because I come from rednecks, and my people invented square dancing. Which means we're so bad at it, we have to have someone tell us what to do, as we're doing it.

— Steve Neal

I went to a liberal arts college where a required class was "The History of Dance." But I was annoyed that the professor had so little knowledge of the lap dance. Come on, I'm paying a lot of money to go to school here, know your subject.

— Tony Deyo

* DATING *

When women don't want to give out their phone number, they make up a number. This one girl said to me, "My telephone number? 4,5,6 - 7,8,9,10." "Is that by any chance in the 1,2,3 area code?"

— Ron Richards

I was in a club the other night. A woman actually asked me out. She said, "You — out!"

— Steve Smith

I saw a personal ad that looked interesting. It said she loved long walks, running on the beach, going to parks. As it turns out, she was a German shepherd.

— David Corrado

I have bad luck with women. A woman I was dating told me on the phone, "I have to go, there's a tele-marketer on the other line."

— Zach Galifiankis

I'd just like to meet a girl with a head on her shoulders. I hate necks.

— Steve Martin

I guess I'm looking for a woman like my mother, and on our first date she'd put her breast in my mouth.

— Adam Sandler

I asked this one girl out and she said, "You got a friend?" I said yes, she said, "Then go out with him."

— Dom Irrera

What is a date really, but a job interview that lasts all night? The only difference is that in not many job interviews is there a chance you'll wind up naked.

— **Jerry Seinfeld**

Dating is a lot like sports. You have to practice, you work out, you study the greats. You hope to make the team, and it hurts to be cut.

— **Sinbad**

I hate first dates. I made the mistake of telling my date a lie about myself and she caught me. I didn't think she'd actually demand to see the bat cave.

— **Alex Reed**

It costs a lot of money to date. I took a girl out to dinner the other night. I said, "What'll you have?" She said, "I guess I'll have the steak and lobster." I said, "Guess again."

— **Skip Stephenson**

Why does a guy say "I'm seeing her" when he really means "I'm touching her"?

— **Jason Love**

An average guy makes a date with a girl. It costs him one hundred dollars, two hundred dollars. I make a date with a girl, it costs me nothing. I come up to her house. She wants to go out. I let her go! What's my business? I have to follow her around?

— Jackie Mason

Dating is tough. I went out with a girl last week who had two kids from five different fathers.

— Erik Mackenroth

I had a lady up in my apartment the other night. She gave me the classic line all girls give guys on the first date, "Steve, if we do anything tonight we won't be friends." I said, "Hell, I'll find new friends."

— Steve Smith

Each person has their own sexual timetable of what should happen when. We need some sort of rule-book: standard dating procedure. "We've been out three times. According to Article 7, Section 5, there's got to be some physical contact. Otherwise, I will report you to the board, and they can put out a warrant for an embrace."

— Jerry Seinfeld

I don't get no respect. A girl phoned me and said, "Come on over, there's nobody home." I went over. Nobody was home.

— Rodney Dangerfield

I was on a date, and this girl teased a banana in a suggestive manner, and said, "That could be you." I replied, "Well then, I should probably get that dark, soft-spot looked at."

— *Deric Harrington*

I'm dating again, which is very exciting because I'm married.

— **Mike Dugan**

* DEATH *

I want to die with a smile on my face. Hopefully, it won't be mine.

— **Matt Vance**

An undertaker calls a son-in-law, "About your mother-in-law, should we embalm her, cremate her, or bury her?" He says, "Do all three. Don't take chances."

— **Myron Cohen**

The upshot to dying is that you don't have to go to work the next day.

— *Jason Love*

One of my big fears in life is that I'm going to die and my parents are going to have to clear out my apartment and find that porno wing I've been adding on for years. There'll be more than one funeral that day.

— **Bill Hicks**

A new study found that one in 500 men will die from having sex. That's why we rush through it, we might die!

— **Jay Leno**

Before he died, my father asked to be cremated and have his ashes spread on a golf course. I put him in a sand trap. He could never get out of the bunkers when he was alive, now he's spending eternity there.

— **Jeff Jena**

Just as the prisoner was being strapped into the electric chair, the priest said, "Son, is there anything I can do for you?" The prisoner said, "Yeah, when they pull the switch, hold my hand."

— **Dick Gregory**

Dr. Kevorkian is onto something. I think he's great. Because suicide is our way of saying to God, "You can't fire me. I quit."

— **Bill Maher**

Sometimes I think I'd be better off dead. No, wait. Not me, you.

— **Emo Philips**

You know you're on a diet when cat food commercials make you hungry.

— **Andy Bumatai**

I have a great diet. You're allowed to eat anything you want, but you must eat it with naked fat people.

— **Ed Bluestone**

Trying to convince your wife you're sticking to your diet? Eat the whole cake, leftovers will only prove you've been snacking.

— **Bill Cosby**

I was on the grapefruit diet. For breakfast I ate fifteen grapefruit. Now when I go to the bathroom I keep squirting myself in the eye.

— **Max Alexander**

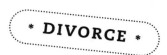

* DIVORCE *

It is a sad fact that fifty percent of marriages in this country end in divorce. But hey, the other half end in death. You could be one of the lucky ones!

— *Richard Jeni*

Divorce comes from the old Latin word *divorcerum*, meaning "having your genitals torn out through your wallet." And the judge said, "All the money, and we'll just shorten it to 'alimony.'"

— *Robin Williams*

My ex-wife is going back to court to get more money, and my lawyer asks, "Are you all right with that?" And I go, "Yeah. I was just going to blow that money on food and shelter."

— *Rocky LaPorte*

Divorce is painful. There's an easy way to save yourself a lot of trouble. Just find a woman you hate and buy her a house.

— *Pat Paulsen*

My wife and I had an amicable divorce. She lets me see my stuff on weekends. Last Sunday I took my sweaters to Disneyland.

— *Craig Shoemaker*

The difference between divorce and legal separation is that a legal separation gives a husband time to hide his money.

— *Johnny Carson*

With my wife I don't get no respect. I told her when I die, I want to be cremated. She's planning a barbeque.

— *Rodney Dangerfield*

My wife left me. I should have seen it coming: for the past year she called me her insignificant other. By the end of the marriage, her favorite position was man on top, woman visiting her mother.

— *Daniel Liebert*

What happened to my marriage? It was broken up by my mother-in-law. My wife came home from work early and she found us in bed together.

— *Lenny Bruce*

My first wife divorced me because I didn't match her shoes. I was a lazy white loafer.

— *Kelly Monteith*

It wasn't actually a divorce. I was traded.

— *Tim Conway*

It's tough. After five years of marriage, it's difficult to lose the one with the good credit rating.

— **Rich Voss**

I've had a helluva year. My wife just left me, and I'm going through a sex change: I'm turning back into a man.

— **Danny Liebert**

When I got divorced, that was group sex. My wife screwed me in front of the jury.

— **Rodney Dangerfield**

* DOCTORS *

I hate the waiting room, so sometimes I start screwing around with the stuff. Take all the tongue depressors out, lick them, put them back. Two can play at this waiting game.

— **Jerry Seinfeld**

Be suspicious of any doctor who tries to take your temperature with his finger.

— **David Letterman**

I said, "Doctor, it hurts when I do this." He said, "Then don't do that!"

— **Henny Youngman**

I just went for my annual physical and the doctor
told me to take a stress test. So I called my mother.

— Craig Sharf

I went to a doctor and told him, "My penis is burning."
He said, "That means somebody is talking about it."

— Garry Shandling

I went to bed with an ophthalmologist, who asked,
"Is it better like this? Or like that?"

— Tommy Koenig

* DOGS *

They say a dog is man's best friend, but I don't buy it.
How many of your friends have had you neutered?

— Larry Reeb

I just bought a Chihuahua. It's the dog for lazy people.
You don't have to walk it. Just hold it out the window
and squeeze.

— Anthony Clark

I like all animals, but those really large poodles are just ridiculously fu-fu looking. They're like canine drag queens. Except if you get attacked by a large poodle, their wig doesn't fall off, and they don't hit you with a size 16 red pump.

— Steve Neal

I like Yorkshire terriers. They're good to wash your car with. They fit right in the bucket, which is good. "Hold your breath," *swoosh!* Then you get a blow dryer, put a stick up their butts and dust the furniture.

— Billium Coronel

A lot of people walk their dogs and I see them walking along with their little poop bags. If aliens are watching this through telescopes, they're going to think the dogs are the leaders of the planet. If you see two life forms, one of them is making a poop, the other one's carrying it for him, who would you assume is in charge?

— Jerry Seinfeld

They have dog food for constipated dogs. If your dog is constipated, why screw up a good thing? Stay indoors and let 'em bloat.

— David Letterman

My friend George walked his dog, all at once. Walked him from Boston to Fort Lauderdale, and said, "Now you're done."

— Steven Wright

I tell ya, my dog is lazy. He don't chase cars. He sits on the curb and takes down license plate numbers.

— Rodney Dangerfield

Dogs are gross, they drink out of the toilet. But when you're going to the bathroom, maybe your dog is thinking, "Hey, hey, hey — I drink out of that thing! Why don't you just go in my dish, and save yourself a walk down the hallway?"

— Garry Shandling

My dog has started to receive free roll-over minutes.

— Jay London

Some dog I got. We call him Egypt because in every room he leaves a pyramid. His favorite bone is in my arm. Last night he went on the paper four times, three of those times I was reading it.

— Rodney Dangerfield

I sent my dog to obedience school and she liked it. Now she wants to get tied up and whipped.

— Ed Bluestone

I don't need to drink to have a good time, I need to drink to stop the voices in my head.

— Dave Attell

I drink too much. Last time I gave a urine sample there was an olive in it.

— Rodney Dangerfield

Want to have fun when you're the designated driver? Do what I do. At the end of the evening, drop people off at strangers' houses. "Go on in Bob, kiss the wife for me."

— Jay Leno

You walk out of a bar into daylight, if you're nineteen and you stay up all night, it's a victory. But if you're over thirty, then the sun is God's flashlight. We all say the same prayer then, "I swear: I will never do this again as long as I live." And some of us have that little addition, "And this time: I mean it!"

— Larry Miller

Don't drink and drive. Instead, the next time you get too drunk to drive, walk into a local Dominos and order a pizza. Then when they go to deliver it, ask for a ride home.

— Todd Glass

I can't hold my liquor in the winter. I'm pretty sure it's the mittens.

— Jonathan Katz

* DRIVING *

Driving a crappy car changes your entire mindset. If someone cuts me off on the freeway I can't flip them off, because I may need that guy to jump-start me in a few minutes.

— Dobie Maxwell

Whenever I pick up a hitchhiker I say, "Put your seat belt on, I want to try something I saw in a cartoon."

— Steven Wright

My mom taught me how to drive. I can't drive worth a damn, but I can change all my clothes at a stoplight.

— Craig Shoemaker

I remember learning to drive on my dad's lap. Did you guys ever do that? He'd work the brakes. I'd work the wheel. Then I went to take the driver's test and sat on the examiner's lap. I failed the exam, but he still writes me.

— *Garry Shandling*

Have you noticed? Anybody going slower than you is an idiot, and anyone going faster than you is a moron.

— *George Carlin*

Fear is being stuck in traffic and you just had two cups of coffee and a bran muffin.

— *John Mendoza*

I was stopped once for doing 53 in a 35-mile-per hour zone, but I got off. I told them I had dyslexia.

— *Spanky*

The cop asked how fast I was going. I said, "All I know is I spilled beer all over my hooker."

— *Craig Kilborn*

When I'm driving I see a sign that says, "Caution: Small Children Playing." I slow down, and then it occurs to me: I'm not afraid of small children.

— Jonathan Katz

One time a cop pulled me over for running a stop sign. He said, "Didn't you see the stop sign?" I said, "Yeah, but I don't believe everything I read."

— Steven Wright

I was pulled over in Massachusetts for reckless driving. The judge asked me, "Do you know what the punishment for drunk driving in this state is?" I said, "I don't know. Reelection to the Senate?"

— Emo Philips

I used to have a girlfriend who would blow me when I drove. It wasn't every time I drove, but every time I drove into a tree.

— Adam Richmond

* DRUGS *

I used to do drugs. I still do drugs. But I used to, too.

— **Mitch Hedberg**

I recently attended a pro-drug rally, in my basement.

— **David Cross**

I would never advocate the use of dope. Because I'm not a professional athlete, and I can't get my hands on the good stuff.

— **Greg Proops**

You should always say no to drugs. That will drive the prices down.

— **Geechy Guy**

The War on Drugs is a big waste of money. The government is pissing it away just so they can put on a big show for the people who are against drugs, because those people happen to vote. I don't think marijuana smokers get to the voting booth as often as they'd like to. "What, it was yesterday?"

— **Drew Carey**

Why is there such controversy about drug testing? I know plenty of guys who'd be willing to test any drug they can come up with.

— George Carlin

Drugs don't enhance your creativity. You get the same old results with heroin. Your neighbors will complain when the ambulance shows up like clockwork. The firemen are going to track footprints on the rug. Your baby's going to keep waking up because of the guy shouting, "1, 2, 3 — clear!" And you always lose your job. Your boss says, "It happened on Monday and twice on Tuesday — you died. We can't have that here, there are plenty of other bike messengers."

— Paul Alexander

A recent government study reported that eight percent of full-time employees are on drugs at work. I think this study is flawed. The figure is too low. Because that eight percent are only the people so stoned they answered yes to the question.

— Bill Maher

I've asked, "What is it about cocaine that makes it so wonderful?" And they say, "It intensifies your personality." But what if you're an asshole?

— Bill Cosby

* EMOTIONS *

Men only have two feelings, we're either hungry or horny. I tell my wife, if I don't have an erection, make me a sandwich.

— **Bobby Slayton**

Share your feelings with your woman. And she'll leave you for a guy who never cries and who spanks her.

— **Jim Carrey**

What is guilt? Guilt is the pledge drive constantly hammering in our heads that keeps us from fully enjoying the show. Guilt is the reason they put the articles in *Playboy*.

— **Dennis Miller**

* EMPLOYMENT *

Black unemployment is up fifty percent of the time. That's not a bad thing, because the last time we were fully employed, we didn't have benefits like freedom.

— **Shang**

My boss told me to get my ass in gear, but I told him I'm shiftless.

— **Jay London**

This one job said they wanted a college degree or equivalent. I said, "Perfect, I have eight years of high school."

— **Buzz Nutley**

American workers work the first three hours every day just to pay their taxes. So that's why we can't get anything done in the morning; we're government employees!

— **Jay Leno**

A guy in a dirty movie is a man with a giant member whose job it is to have sex with beautiful women, and then get paid. Are you ever late for this job? He's on time every day! He's hopping to work like this, "High-ho, high-ho, it's off to work I go. Good morning everybody, how the hell are you! Coffee? *No!* Let's get right to it!"

— **Richard Jeni**

Most people don't know what they're doing, and a lot of them are really good at it.

— **George Carlin**

A study came out this week that said one out of four American workers is angry at work. And the other three save it for the loved ones at home.

— **Bill Maher**

There are many ways to know that you have a bad job. For instance, if you have to carry out the body of the guy whose place you're taking. Or, if you're employed at the post office next to a coworker who's constantly muttering under his breath, and the only word you can make out is your name.

— Dennis Miller

Collaborative, from the Greek *col*: with other people; *laborative*: the other people are morons.

— Richard Jeni

I hated my last boss. He asked, "Why are you two hours late?" I said, "I fell downstairs." He said, "That doesn't take two hours."

— Johnny Carson

My father is semi-retired. He goes half-way to work, and then he comes home.

— Tommy Koenig

When you go to work if your name is on the building, you're rich. If you're name is on your desk, you're middle-class. If your name is on your shirt, you're poor.

— **Rich Hall**

In a survey, two out of three women said they'd had sex with someone in their office. I can't even get the toner cartridge to go in the copier.

— **Jay Leno**

You moon the wrong person at an office party and suddenly you're not "professional" any more.

— **Jeff Foxworthy**

Most people work just hard enough not to get fired and get paid just enough money not to quit.

— **George Carlin**

I lost my job. No, I didn't really lose my job. I know where my job is, still. It's just when I go there, there's this new guy doing it. I lost my girl. No, I didn't really lose my girl. I know where my girl is, still. It's just when I go there, there's this new guy doing it.

— **Bob Goldthwait**

The problem with unemployment is that the minute you wake up in the morning, you're on the job.

— **Slappy White**

* ENGAGEMENTS *

Many of my friends are getting engaged and are buying diamonds for their fiancées. What better to symbolize marriage than the hardest thing known to man?

— Mike Dugan

My fiancée told me the rule of thumb on how much to spend on an engagement ring was two months' salary. So I moved to Haiti for a couple months, made a buck eighty. Nice plywood ring, no knots. I sanded it myself.

— Barry Kennedy

* ENVIRONMENT *

Underground nuclear testing, defoliation of the rain forests, toxic waste . . . let's put it this way, if the world were a big apartment, we wouldn't get our deposit back.

— John Ross

The environment is screwed up, but you can still have fun. I'm going brown-water rafting this summer.

— Barry Crimmins

Do you ever wonder where all the farts go? They go up into the atmosphere and they form the fart zone. It's right above the ozone layer, and that's why we have to protect the ozone layer!

— **Steve Martin**

I had a Great Earth day. I drove around with my muffler off, flicking butts out the window, then I hit a deer.

— **Drew Carey**

Environmentalists announced this week that two dams on a river in Maine are to be torn down, in an effort to encourage salmon to return to the river to spawn. Also encouraging salmon to spawn: salmon porn.

— **Jimmy Fallon**

* ETHNICITY *

Some people say all black people look alike. We call those people "police."

— **Dave Chappelle**

I love black women, but I like white women, too. That's why I can't hate white men: we need them for breeding.

— **Alonzo Bodden**

I'm extra ghetto, if I do say so myself. I got two six-year-olds, and they ain't twins.

— Corey Holcomb

There's a stereotype that black people are lazy. I don't know if that's true, but I know white people went all the way to Africa to get out of doing work.

— Lance Crouther

Does it matter if someone calls you a Latino or Hispanic? I don't mind Chicano, which is a Mexican-American, but Hispanic I don't like. The U.S. Census Bureau came up with it and who wants to be associated with a word that has "panic" in it?" In a way, it's progress; we used to be "Other."

— George Lopez

* EXERCISE *

Oh yeah, I'll continue to work out. Until I get married.

— Tom Arnold

They say that exercise and proper diet are the keys to a longer life. Oh, well.

— Drew Carey

It takes too long to work out. It's just faster not to walk by a mirror when you're naked.

— Richard Jeni

They say the best exercise takes place in the bedroom. I believe it, because that's where I get the most resistance.

— Jeff Shaw

I ran three miles today. Finally I said, "Lady, take your purse!"

— Emo Philips

I recently started exercising, and I've got to say, Lamaze classes rock! Controlled breathing is my kind of workout. And best of all, I don't have to be embarrassed about my gut. There are some enormous women in that room. It's like they've been eating for two.

— Brian Beatty

I get winded when I use a rotary phone.

— **Jonathan Katz**

If you want to lose weight you have to exercise. I tried, went to the spa. They had this new machine there called Nautilus. I couldn't figure out how it worked, so I just strapped it on, and dragged it around. I'm up to five machines now.

— **Frank D'Amico**

With me nothing comes easy. This morning I did my push-ups in the nude. I didn't see the mousetrap.

— **Rodney Dangerfield**

Last year I entered the Los Angeles marathon. I finished last. It was embarrassing. And the guy who was in front of me, second to last, was making fun of me. He said, "How does it feel to come in last?" I said, "You want to know?" So I dropped out.

— **Gerry Bednob**

A new study says that one of the advantages of the treadmill is that it's the highest calorie burner of the exercises. And the other advantage is that hamsters can now laugh at us.

— **Johnny Robish**

* FAMILY *

There's no such thing as fun for the whole family; there are no massage parlors with ice cream and free jewelry.

— Jerry Seinfeld

My daughter is no bargain. In public school she was voted "Most Likely to Conceive."

— Rodney Dangerfield

I wanted to do something nice for my mother-in-law so I bought her a chair, but they won't let me plug it in.

— Henny Youngman

My brother-in-law is always there for me when he needs a favor.

— David Corrado

I told my mother-in-law to take a trip to the Thousand Islands. I told her, "Spend a week in each island!"

— Henny Youngman

* FANTASIES *

I asked my girlfriend who she fantasized about while we were having sex, and she said, "I don't really have time."

— Owen O'Neill

Last time I tried to make love to my wife, nothing was happening, so I said to her, "What's the matter, you can't think of anybody either?"

— Rodney Dangerfield

* FASHION *

The suit is the universal business outfit for men. I don't know why it projects this image of power. "We'd better do what this guy says, his pants match his jacket!"

— Jerry Seinfeld

I'm glad earth tones are popular again; it means I don't have to do laundry as often.

— Reno Goodale

The worst thing that can happen to a man is to have his wife come home and he has lost the child. "How did everything go?" "Great, we're playing hide and seek and she's winning."

— Sinbad

Now that I'm a dad, I'm sure my father is laughing in his grave. I used to ask my father, "Dad, where did all those wrinkles come from on your face?" "From you, your little brother, and your goddamn sister."

— Jack Coen

My wife just let me know I'm about to become a father for the first time. The bad news is that we already have two kids.

— Brian Kiley

* FATHERS *

When I was born my father spent three weeks trying to find a loophole in my birth certificate.

— *Jackie Vernon*

My father hugged me only once, on my twenty-first birthday. It was very awkward. I now know what it was that made me feel so uncomfortable: the nudity.

— *Ray Romano*

My father refused to spend money on me as a kid. One time I broke my arm playing football and my father tried to get a free X-ray by taking me down to the airport and making me lie down with the luggage.

— *Glenn Super*

According to my dad, he had a really tough childhood. He had to walk twenty miles to school in five feet of snow, and he was only four feet tall.

— *Dana Eagle*

My father used to ground me — and then run electricity through me.

— Taylor Negron

My mother said the best time to ask my dad for anything was during sex. Not the best advice I've ever been given.

— Jimmy Carr

My father didn't ask me to leave home. He took me down to the highway and pointed.

— Henny Youngman

My father's mind is going. He called me and said, "When I get up to go to the bathroom in the middle of the night, I don't have to turn on the light. It goes on automatically when I start, and goes off when I stop." I said, "Dad, you're peeing in the fridge."

— Jonathan Katz

* FINANCES *

It's the people who ask for loans who you don't want to lend money to.

— Jason Love

Strange things happen when you're in debt. Two weeks ago, my car broke down and my phone got disconnected. I was one electric bill away from being Amish.

— **Tom Ryan**

You ever know anybody who bounced a check to pay a bounced check? Yeah, that was me. But what about those fools who let you pay a bounced check with a check? They deserve not to get paid.

— **Herb Clark**

If you had a penny and threw it off the Empire State Building, and it hit somebody in the head, it would kill him. Talk about getting your money's worth.

— **Heywood Banks**

I had a nest egg, but I lost it gambling. I was betting I'd be dead by now.

— **Drew Carey**

Conservatives say if you don't give the rich more money, they will lose their incentive to invest. As for the poor, they tell us they've lost all incentive because we've given them too much money.

— George Carlin

You ever have somebody owe you money, and have the nerve to wear new clothes around you? Brand new clothes, and they point them out like, "Hey, look what I just picked up?" Well, did you see my money while you were down there?

— Chris Rock

There's a fine line between fishing and standing on the shore looking like an idiot.

— Steven Wright

Whoever came up with ice fishing must have had the worst marriage on the planet.

— Jeff Cesario

I used to go fishing until one day it struck me: you can buy fish. What the hell am I doing in a boat at 4:30 in the morning? If I want a hamburger, I don't track cattle down.

— Kenny Rogerson

Fish aren't that smart. For example, I once caught a fish by dangling a worm in the ocean. Shouldn't he have been suspicious when he saw it? I'm not saying I'm a genius, but if I dive into a swimming pool and there's a sausage in the drain, I don't care how hungry I am, I'm going to ask a question or two before I chow down.

— Richard Jeni

I like fishing, but I don't have any patience. So I use an aquarium.

— Craig Sharf

* FLYING *

Some people have the audacity to put a little bolt through their penis. Which makes me think it must be fun at the airport metal detector. "Will you take out your keys? Do you have any other metal on you? Yes? Will you take that out, too?"

— Robin Williams

They confiscated my cigar cutter. What was I going to do, circumcise the pilot?

— Jeffrey Ross

A new machine for passenger screening at airports sees right through clothing. Listen, if it keeps the screeners awake...

— Conan O'Brien

Did you hear about those two strangers who were arrested for having sex in first class on American Airlines? You know who I feel sorry for? The guy in the middle seat

— Jay Leno

If you're in the mile high club, but got there by yourself, does that only count for half a mile?

— Larry Getlen

Hooters Air is off the ground. In the event of a water landing, there'll be a wet t-shirt contest.

— Craig Kilborn

A Florida airline is starting nude flights. Passengers are allowed one carry-on and one strap-on.

— Conan O'Brien

A new airline in Chile is providing two prostitutes for each first-class passenger. You have to call them hookers. If you call them stewardesses, it's sexist.

— Jay Leno

* FOOD *

I want Baskin-Robbins to develop a cone that licks back.

— Johnny Carson

I like cinnamon rolls, but I don't always have time to make a pan. That's why I wish they would sell cinnamon roll incense. After all, I'd rather light a stick and have my roommate wake up with false hopes.

— Mitch Hedberg

I went to the Erotic Bakery today and got something that really turned my lady on: a cake in the shape of my wallet.

— Craig Kilborn

Scientists say that chocolate affects your brain the same way sex does. Which means that after they eat a Snickers, guys roll over and go to sleep. And women ask the wrapper, "What are you thinking?"

— Jim Wyatt

I love pizza better than sex. Of course that's only because I can get pizza.

— Doug Graham

Someone said to me, "Make yourself a sandwich." Well, if I could make myself a sandwich, I wouldn't make myself a sandwich. I'd make myself a horny, 18-year-old billionaire.

— George Carlin

In football the object is for the quarterback to be on target with his aerial assault. With short bullet passes and long bombs, he marches his troops into enemy territory with a sustained ground attack that punches holes in the forward wall of the enemy's defensive line. In baseball, the object is to go home, and to be safe. "I hope I'll be safe at home."

— George Carlin

The hardest part of being a professional football player is: on the one hand you're a millionare, on the other, they blow a whistle and you have to run around after a football. To me, the whole idea of being a millionare is: somebody throws a football at me — maybe I catch it, maybe I don't. I'd think you could get someone to hand you the ball, at that point.

— Jerry Seinfeld

The NFL cheerleaders are gorgeous and sexy, but are their cheers helping anybody? Ever see a player interviewed after the game say, "We were down pretty big in the fourth quarter, but then the cheerleaders started chanting 'Defense!' That's when it dawned on the coach, 'Them gals are right!'"

— Gary Gulman

According to a new survey, seventy-six percent of men would rather watch a football game than have sex. My question is, why do we have to choose? Why do you think they invented half-time?

— **Jay Leno**

Super Bowl Sunday is the one day of the year where everyone in the country, regardless of their religious beliefs, completely stops what they're normally doing. Especially the team I'm rooting for.

— **Dennis Miller**

* FRIENDSHIPS *

You got friends, then you've got your best friend. Big difference. To me, a friend is a guy who will help you move. A best friend is a guy who will help you move a body.

— **Dave Attell**

My best friend ran away with my wife. I really miss him.

— Henny Youngman

* FURNITURE *

My favorite furniture brand is the La-Z-Boy. This is very flattering to the prospective customer, isn't it? Why don't we just call it the "Half-conscious deadbeat with no job, home all day, eating Cheetos and watching TV" recliner?

— Jerry Seinfeld

* GAMBLING *

A man went to Las Vegas with a $30,000 Cadillac and came home on a $100,000 bus.

— Henny Youngman

A man wins the lottery. He says to his wife, "I've got it made! Start packing." She says, "Am I packing for cold weather or warm?" He says, "How the hell should I know? Just be out by the time I get back."

— Red Buttons

* GARDENING *

If you water it and it dies, it's a plant. If you pull it out and it grows back, it's a weed.

— Gallagher

When my wife asked me to start a garden, the first thing I dug up was an excuse.

— Henny Youngman

All the plants in my house are dead; I shot them last night. I was teasing them by watering them with ice cubes.

— Steven Wright

* GASOLINE *

I bought a gallon of gas, as an investment.

— Jay Leno

Gasoline may go to $3 a gallon to cover the ever-increasing cost of screwing us.

— Craig Kilborn

I'm the only person I know who ran out of gas at a car wash. I've also run out of gas at a drive-thru window at one a.m. I had to push the car five feet, wait for someone to make an order, push it another five feet, wait for someone else to make an order, push it another five feet to give my order, and buy something for the tow truck driver, too.

— Dobie Maxwell

* GHOSTS *

More women believe in ghosts than men. They've had experience. They have sex with a guy. They turn around, and he's vanished.

— Jay Leno

* GIRLFRIENDS *

You can't please everybody. Like, I have a girlfriend. My girlfriend to me is the most wonderful, most remarkable person in the world. That's to me. But to my wife . . .

— Jackie Mason

A girlfriend is just like a wife, except you have sex with her.

— Jason Love

My girlfriend is not a ball and chain, she's more of a spring-loaded trap.

— Kevin Hench

I don't have a girlfriend. But I do know a woman who'd be mad at me for saying that.

— Mitch Hedberg

* GOD *

Guilt is simply God's way of letting you know that you're having too good a time.

— Dennis Miller

If I had the power of God, I would use it to open my CDs.

— Jim Carrey

What if God's a woman? Not only am I going to hell, I'll never know why.

— Adam Ferrara

* GOLF *

If you watch a game, it's fun. If you play it, it's recreation. If you work at it, it's golf.

— Bob Hope

I'm into golf now. I'm getting pretty good. I can almost hit the ball as far as I can throw the clubs.

— Bob Ettinger

I played golf. I did not get a hole in one, but I did hit a guy. That's way more satisfying.

— Mitch Hedberg

While playing golf today I hit two good balls. I stepped on a rake.

— Henny Youngman

I don't rent a golf cart. I don't need one. Where I hit the ball, I can use public transportation.

— **Gene Perret**

Golf is one of the few sports where a white man can dress like a black pimp.

— **Robin Williams**

I play golf even though I hate it. I'm not done with the game yet. I hate those windmills.

— **Mark Guido**

Anyone can be a golf announcer. All you have to do is use that voice you use when you call in sick at work. "I won't be coming in today, I have a golf game to announce."

— **Mike Rowe**

Playing golf the other day I broke 70. That's a lot of clubs.

— Henny Youngman

* GRANDFATHERS *

I played with my grandfather a lot when I was a kid. He was dead, but my parents had him cremated and put his ashes in my Etch-a-Sketch.

— Alan Havey

When I was little my grandfather one Christmas gave me a box of broken glass. He gave my brother a box of Band-Aids, and said, "You two share."

— Steven Wright

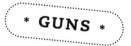

* GUNS *

You have to wait ten days to buy a gun in Los Angeles. I can't stay mad that long.

— Emo Philips

The NRA has their cute little bumper sticker, "You'll get my gun when you pry it from my cold dead hands." Whatever. In a perfect world.

— Dennis Miller

Of course we need firearms. You never know when some nut is going to come up to you and say something like, "You're fired." You gotta be ready.

— Dave Attell

* HAIR *

This is the kind of thing would bum out any young guy. I just found out my father lost his hair — in a slap fight.

— Vernon Chapman

I don't consider myself bald. I'm simply taller than my hair.

— Thom Sharp

All your friends are like, "Hey Dave, is that a bald spot, or what?" "No, friend, it's a blowhole. I'm a dolphin."

— Dave Attell

A study found that the drug for male pattern baldness also lowers the risk of prostate cancer. The bad thing is that you grow hair on your prostate. Now there's a really bad comb-over.

— Jay Leno

A man goes to a barbershop and asks, "How many ahead of me?" "Five." The man leaves. He comes back tomorrow, and asks, "How many ahead of me." "Four." The man leaves. He comes back the next day and asks, "How many ahead of me?" "Six." The man leaves, and the barber says to another, "Follow that guy!" The man comes back and says, "He goes to your house."

— **Henny Youngman**

It's great to have gray hair. Ask anyone who's bald.

— **Rodney Dangerfield**

Hair replacement techniques mean your wife's running her fingers through your hair while you're not at home.

— **Richard Jeni**

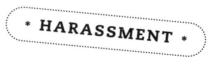

* HARASSMENT *

No means no. So does pepper spray.

— **Jason Love**

Honking the horn at a woman amazes me. What's she supposed to do? Kick off the heels, start running after, hang on to the bumper? "It's a good thing you honked, or I wouldn't have known how you felt."

— Jerry Seinfeld

I'm walking down the street, and a bunch of construction workers working on a building are whistling down at women. I pretend they're whistling at me and I wave back, shake a little hip. They throw their Thermos bottles at me, I sell them on eBay. I think that makes me the winner.

— Basil White

* HEALTH *

Doctors say an active sex life can help a person lead a healthier and longer life. Here's my question: where are you supposed to get that prescription filled?

— Jay Leno

I think tobacco and alcohol warnings are too general. They should be more to the point: "People who smoke will eventually cough up brown pieces of lung." And, "Warning! Alcohol will turn you into the same asshole your father was."

— George Carlin

* HEALTH CLUBS *

Joined a health club last year, spent four hundred bucks. Haven't lost a pound. Apparently, you have to show up.

— Rich Ceisler

Health club patrons, men with breasts the size of lobby furniture.

— Richard Jeni

* HEIGHT *

When I was a kid, I was so short I had to blow my nose through my fly.

— Rodney Dangerfield

* HEROS *

Our heros used to be Teddy Roosevelt and Babe Ruth. Today it's different, we worship political blowhards and overpaid sports figures.

— Vinny Badabing

* HETEROSEXUALITY *

Some men are heterosexual and some men are bisexual and some men don't think about sex at all . . . you know, they become lawyers.

— *Woody Allen*

You're born a heterosexual. It's not a choice. Who would choose this? The guilt, the shame...and do you think I'm *happy* having to hire a decorator?

— *Garry Shandling*

* HISTORY *

Researchers say Stonehenge was built in the form of the female sex organ. No wonder it's baffled men for five thousand years.

— *Jay Leno*

Based on what you know about him in history books, what do you think Abraham Lincoln would be doing if he were alive today? 1. Writing his memoirs of the Civil War. 2. Advising the President. 3. Desperately clawing at the inside of his coffin.

— *David Letterman*

I joined a Civil War reenactment club. Next weekend, we're burning down Atlanta.

— Craig Sharf

You don't know who to believe. Like Abraham Lincoln. Abe Lincoln said all men are created equal. He never went to a nude beach.

— Rodney Dangerfield

* HOLIDAYS *

Hallmark is coming out with a new card for guys who forget Valentine's Day. The card is small and gold and maxes out at ten grand.

— Craig Kilborn

Valentine's Day. Or, as men like to call it: extortion Day.

— Jay Leno

A Valentine's Day survey found 39% of women say a man doesn't have to pay for the dinner. It all depends on how comfortable he is with masturbation.

— Conan O'Brien

Mother's Day is the day we honor the woman we blame for all our personal problems.

— David Letterman

Father's Day, when you get that lethal combination of alcohol and new power tools.

— David Letterman

Last Halloween was bad for me. I got real beat up. I went to a party dressed as a piñata.

— Jim Samuels

When I was a kid my parents always sent me out as a tramp: high heel shoes, fishnet stockings...

— David Letterman

When I was in college, I came up with the perfect Halloween costume. I wore cat ears and angel wings and carried a pitch fork, and went as every girl on campus.

— Steve Hofstetter

On Halloween I ran out of candy and had to give the kids nicotine gum.

— David Letterman

I celebrated Thanksgiving in the traditional way. I invited everyone in my neighborhood to my house, we had an enormous feast. And then I killed them and took their land.

— Jon Stewart

You can tell you ate too much for Thanksgiving when you have to let your bathrobe out.

— Jay Leno

Women get a little more excited about New Year's Eve than men do. It's like an excuse, you get drunk, you make a lot of promises you're not going to keep, the next morning as soon as you wake up you start breaking them. For men, we just call that a date.

— Jay Leno

* HOMOSEXUALITY *

The sodomy laws have been overturned, so now we can overturn each other.

— Craig Kilborn

The Supreme Court has ruled that sex between two men is legal, and sex between two women is exciting.

— Conan O'Brien

The Kinsey Institute says gay men have bigger sex organs. Hence the origin of gay pride.

— Jay Leno

They say you can't tell guys are gay just by looking. But if two guys are kissing, you can figure at least one of them is gay.

— Bill Braudis

I'm in favor of gay marriage. Then at least both people are excited about planning the wedding.

— Jay Leno

I was once involved in a same-sex marriage. There was the same sex over and over and over.

— David Letterman

In college I experimented with heterosexuality: I slept with a straight guy. I was really drunk.

— Bob Smith

I could never be gay, it's depressing enough being rejected by women.

Robert Wuhl

Paris has started a campaign to attract more gay tourists. First, they're rolling two giant boulders to the foot of the Eiffel Tower.

— Conan O'Brien

We're single guys, nobody washes dishes. I had to go to the closet and get the Yahtzee game, to find a clean cup to drink out of.

— **Dobie Maxwell**

According to a study in *McCall's* magazine, the sexiest thing a man can say to a woman is, "Let me do the dishes." This is what I hate about these magazines, they set impossible standards.

— **Jay Leno**

Even though women work all day long, they still come home and clean up about ninety-nine percent of the things cleaned up around the house. There is still a problem here. Women aren't as proud of their ninety-nine percent as men are of their one percent.

We clean up something, we're going to talk about it all week long. It might be on the news.

— Jeff Foxworthy

Men leave their socks lying around because we can use them for oven mitts.

— Mike Dugan

✷ HOUSING ✷

I can't believe I actually own my own house. I'm looking at a house, it's five hundred grand. The Realtor says, "It's got a great view." For five hundred grand I better open up the curtains and see breasts against the window.

— Garry Shandling

I just bought a new house. I don't want to brag, but it's in a golf-course community. A famous golf course, you may have heard of, the Putt-Putt. It's a beautiful place: my deck overlooks the 3rd, 4th, 7th, 12th, 15th fairways, the windmill, and the clown's mouth. I'm living the dream.

— Tony Deyo

My idea of the perfect living room would be the bridge on the Starship Enterprise. Big chair, nice screen, remote control. *Star Trek* was the ultimate male fantasy: hurtling through space in your living room, watching TV. That's why the aliens were always dropping in, Kirk had the big screen.

— Jerry Seinfeld

Roommates are tough. Even if you shared an apartment with the Pope, I guarantee that three weeks into it you'd be going, "Hey, you mind picking up the cape, man? And quit leaving the papal miter on the kitchen counter."

— Jeff Foxworthy

The only good thing about a singles' apartment is that you never had to clean it up. At least not until the day you moved and tried to get the security deposit back. Then you'd argue with the landlord. "No sir, the back door was missing when we moved in here. The pizzas were always on the ceiling."

— Jeff Foxworthy

* HUSBANDS *

Men are married about six months, and they can't even dress themselves anymore, "Honey, does this tie go with my underwear?"

— John Mendoza

I was a teacher for awhile, but now I'm a full-time stay-at-home Dad. I'm not ashamed of it, a lot of guys do it. The only difference between me and them is, I don't have any kids.

— Tony Deyo

I don't see myself as a married guy. I still see myself as a pirate.

— Adam Ferrara

* ILLNESSES *

A woman woke up from four and a half years in a coma. Her husband spent the whole time by her bedside, and when she came to, he said, "Honey, can you get me a beer?"

— Jay Leno

Ever get one of those ice cream headaches? You know, when you tell your girlfriend she's gaining weight, and she hits you with the scoop? "Ow! I said that too fast!"

— **Jeff Shaw**

This morning I found a spider in my bed, and I thought, "Gee, I must have been drunk."

— **Fred Wolf**

Some women think that any aerosol can kill a bug. My wife says, "Deodorant! Use that! I've killed bugs with deodorant!" Try killing a monster with deodorant, it's not easy, and all I could find was the roll-on.

— **Ray Romano**

The stick insect has sex for 79 days straight. If it's only been 77 days, is that a quickie? And you know that even after 79 days, the female goes, "Oh, so close!" And the guy tells his buddies it was 158 days.

— **Jay Leno**

* INSTRUCTIONS *

I once went to Sears to buy a workbench. It came in
a big, big box and there was some assembly required.
There were instructions, but I didn't need those. Hey,
I'm a guy; my balls will tell me how it all fits together.

— *Tim Allen*

* INSURANCE *

My wife and I took out life insurance policies on one
another, so now it's just a waiting game.

— *Bil Dwyer*

* INTERNET *

Congress says that half of Americans use the
Internet. The other half has sex with real partners.

— *Jay Leno*

Thanks to the Internet I had my identity stolen a few
months ago, and my credit actually improved. I'm
dating now, have a new car. Life is good.

— *Steve Moris*

The Federal Trade Commission says two-thirds of spam has false or misleading information. Thanks for nothing, Penis Extender.

— Conan O'Brien

According to a survey, 85 percent of men admit they surf the Internet wearing nothing but their underwear. Sixty-three percent said that's how they lost their last job.

— Jay Leno

* JEWELRY *

A recent marketing poll shows that 32% of all diamonds are purchased right before Christmas. And 50% are purchased right after the test strip turns pink.

— Conan O'Brien

When I was a boy my mother wore a mood ring. When she was in a good mood it turned blue. In a bad mood, it left a big red mark on my forehead.

— Jeff Shaw

★ LAUGHTER ★

If you can laugh at yourself loud and hard every time you fall, people will think you're drunk.

— Conan O'Brien

★ LAZINESS ★

I had a lazy eye as a kid, and it gradually spread to my whole body.

— Tom Cotter

My uncle's so lazy he married a girl who was already pregnant.

— Rodney Dangerfield

* LEGS *

A girl's legs are her best friends, but the best of friends must part.

— Redd Foxx

* LESBIANS *

A lesbian is any woman who doesn't like me.

— Jason Love

A study claims that the relative lengths of the index and ring fingers indicates whether a woman is a lesbian. If between her thumb and index finger is another woman's nipple, that's an even better indication.

— Bill Maher

A new study claims that teenage lesbians have a higher chance of smoking than straight girls. Another study also reveals that guys who do studies would rather study teenage lesbians than almost anything else in the world.

— Jay Leno

* LISTENING *

Scientists say a woman listens with her whole brain, while a man only listens with half his brain. The other half is picturing her naked.

— Jay Leno

Women don't want to hear what you think. Women want to hear what they think, in a deeper voice.

— Bill Cosby

* LOVE *

What is love? An extension of like. What is lust? An extension.

— Rodney Dangerfield

A guy knows he's in love when he loses interest in his car for a couple of days.

— Tim Allen

A lot of people wonder how you know if you're really in love. Just ask yourself this one question: "Would I mind being financially destroyed by this person?"

— Ronnie Shakes

I've been in love with the same woman for forty-one years. If my wife finds out, she'll kill me.

— Henny Youngman

The difference between love and sex is that sex relieves tension and love causes it.

— Woody Allen

* MAGAZINES *

There's very little advice in men's magazines, because men don't think there's a lot they don't know. Women want to learn. Men think, "I know what I'm doing, just show me somebody naked."

— Jerry Seinfeld

In Ohio, a sixth-grade boy was suspended for three days for bringing the *Sports Illustrated* swimsuit issue to school with him. That's how you punish a 13-year-old boy: send him home for three days with the *Sports Illustrated* swimsuit issue. Then what, lock him in the bathroom?

— Jay Leno

I read *Cosmopolitan* magazine because I feel like I'm getting a glimpse of the opposing team's game plan.

— Jack Coen

My father says, "Marry a girl who has the same beliefs as the family." I said, "Dad, why would I want a girl who thinks I'm a schmuck?"

— Adam Sandler

Married or single? I have to compare the disadvantages of each. You've got to say to yourself, "Hey, do I want to stay a single guy, and run around in bars with a bunch of different morons? Or, do I want to be married with a family, and stay home with the exact same group of morons?"

— Richard Jeni

I've never been married. I'd like to find that special someone I can grow old with. Someone I can nurture. Someone who can straighten out my finances.

— Mike Dugan

I'd marry the right girl. Someone beautiful, successful and independent who only wants to talk about me.

— Richard Jeni

You know what I did before I married? Anything I wanted to.

— Henny Youngman

The first part of our marriage was very happy. But then, on the way back from the ceremony . . .

— **Henny Youngman**

All men make mistakes, but married men find out about them sooner.

— **Red Skelton**

I love being married. I was single for a long time, and I just got so sick of finishing my own sentences.

— **Brian Kiley**

We were married for better or worse. I couldn't have done better and she couldn't have done worse.

— **Henny Youngman**

Marriage is real tough because you have to deal with feelings, and lawyers.

— **Richard Pryor**

After seven years of marriage, I'm sure of two things: first, never wallpaper together; and second, you'll need two bathrooms, both for her.

— **Dennis Miller**

A man doesn't know what real happiness is until he's married. Then it's too late.

— Henny Youngman

Being happily married is like having a shit job with people you dig.

— Jack Coen

Never, ever, discount the idea of marriage. Sure, someone might tell you that marriage is just a piece of paper. Well, so is money, and what's more life-affirming than cold, hard cash?

— Dennis Miller

A man is incomplete until he's married. Then he's really finished.

— Henny Youngman

My wife wouldn't live with me before we were married. Now that we've been married for 15 years I'm trying to talk her into getting her own place again.

— Jeff Jena

They say married men live longer. It just seems longer.

— Bobby Slayton

Marriage is a good deal like taking a bath: not so hot once you get accustomed to it.

— Henny Youngman

Marriage is give and take. You'd better give it to her or she'll take it away.

— Joey Adams

If your wife doesn't treat you right, stay with her anyway. There's no better way of punishing her.

— Henny Youngman

I tell ya, my wife, we get along good because we have our own arrangement. I mean, one night a week I go out with the boys, and one night a week, she goes out with the boys.

— Rodney Dangerfield

A woman marries hoping that he will change and he doesn't. A man marries hoping she won't change and she does.

— Joey Bishop

Now, of course, I realize that a mixed marriage means one between a man and a woman.

— Michael Feldman

Marriage is not a man's idea. A woman must have thought of it. Years ago some guy said, "Let me get this straight, honey. I can't sleep with anyone else for the rest of my life, and if things don't work out, you get to keep half my stuff? What a great idea."

— Bobby Slayton

Being married is like getting to have your favorite soft drink any time you want. But only your favorite soft drink. It's monogamous. You feel like a hot drink, you better heat up some Mr. Pibb.

— **Jeff Cesario**

If variety is the spice of life, marriage is the big can of leftover Spam.

— **Johnny Carson**

I have a Y chromosome that makes me ask, "Why get married?" But I wouldn't want to put down marriage as a whole — which it is.

— **Kevin Hench**

When we got married, I told my wife I like sex twice a day. She said, "Me, too." Now we never see each other.

— **Rodney Dangerfield**

When you're single, you're the dictator of your own life: "I give the order to fall asleep on the sofa in the middle of the day!" When married, you're part of a vast decision-making body, and this is if the marriage works. That's what's so painful about divorce: you get impeached and you're not even the president.

— Jerry Seinfeld

For our anniversary, I got my wife one of those fur coat kits. A Velcro coat with a hundred gerbils.

— Tom Arnold

I don't understand couples who break up and get back together, especially couples who divorce and remarry. That's like pouring milk on a bowl of cereal, tasting it and saying, "This milk is sour. Well, I'll put it back in the refrigerator, maybe it will be okay tomorrow."

— Larry Miller

I feel my second marriage has finally prepared me for my first.

— Michael Feldman

I was married for a short time. Just long enough to realize all those comedians weren't joking.

— Daniel Lybra

You know your marriage is in trouble when your wife starts wearing the wedding ring on her middle finger.

— Dennis Miller

Most marriages end in divorce and most divorces end in marriage. In other words, most marriages have sad endings and most divorces have happy endings.

— **Tom Ryan**

If God had intended us not to masturbate he would've made our arms shorter.

— **George Carlin**

You know you have a masturbation problem when certain things won't get in your way, like the hiccups.

— **Zach Galifianakis**

More than 100 men and women gathered in San Francisco to participate in the second annual public Masturbate-A-Thon. Even though a lot of people showed up, I heard it was whack.

— **Jimmy Fallon**

My father told me that jacking off could make me go blind. Then he walked into a wall.

— **Robert Schimmel**

* MEDICAL CARE *

I had general anesthesia. That's so weird. You go to sleep in one room, and then you wake up four hours later in a totally different room. Just like college.

— **Ross Shafer**

I had a cholesterol test: they found bacon.

— **Bob Zany**

I had my cholesterol checked and it's higher than my SATs. I can now get into any college based on my cholesterol check.

— **Garry Shandling**

I just got a vasectomy. I didn't mean to, my pocket-knife opened by mistake.

— **Reno Goodale**

A 385-pound man was admitted to a hospital to have a cell phone removed from his butt. I feel sorry for the guy inside going, "Can you hear me now?"

— **Craig Kilborn**

* MEMORY *

Women don't get mad at you about something you just did. They have precision memory, for everything you've ever done: time, date, place, what you said, and your hand position when you said it. This memory will never crash, it probably keeps ticking after she does. You bury her, and from six feet under you'll hear a muffled shout, "AT THE CHURCH PICNIC, 1985, WHAT KIND OF LOOK WAS THAT YOU GAVE KENESHA, MISTER BIG EYES!"

— Sinbad

* MEN *

Men are superior to women. For one thing, men can urinate from a speeding car.

— Will Durst

Men are pigs. Too bad we own everything.

— Tim Allen

I was talking to a businessman, and I said, "Don't you think most men are little boys?" And he said, "I'm no little boy! I make seventy-five thousand dollars a year." And I said, "Well, the way I look at it, you just have bigger toys."

— Jonathan Winters

Men are liars. We'll lie about lying if we have to. I'm an algebra liar. I figure two good lies make a positive.

— Tim Allen

Men brag about the bad shit that happens. "Tell 'em about the time you got electrocuted." "My feet were wet, man, and I plugged the thing in. I got up and I felt the 'lectric going through me, but something in my mind told my hands, because I was holding a beer, and I didn't drop one drop!"

— George Lopez

My Mom said the only reason men are alive is for lawn care and vehicle maintenance.

— Tim Allen

When men get together there's a lot of ego at stake. Ever see two guys meet each other for the first time? Within five minutes, there's a top-it contest of life achievements. The first guy will say something innocuous like, "When I was a kid, I went to the last game when the Mets won the World Series." The other guy goes, "I went to Woodstock. Sat on a speaker." "I'm on a first-name basis with the Unknown Soldier." "I was the busboy at the Last Supper." "I remember you. How did you like the tip?"

— Joe Bolster

Only a man will think of a burp as a greeting for another man.

— Tim Allen

They say men get sexier as they get older. No, sexy men get sexier as they get older, the rest of us get red sports cars.

— Jeff Shaw

Men and women are a lot alike in certain situations. Like when they're both on fire, they're exactly alike.

— Dave Attell

Men look at women the way men look at cars. Everyone looks at Ferraris. Now and then we like a pickup truck. And we all end up with a station wagon.

— Tim Allen

All plans between men are tentative, if one man should have an opportunity to pursue a woman. It doesn't matter how important the arrangements are: when they scrub a space shuttle, it's because an astronaut met someone on his way to the launch pad. They hold the countdown; he's leaning against the rocket talking to her, "What do you say we get together for some Tang?"

— Jerry Seinfeld

Men think sex is their idea. How stupid of us. Women have already decided when, where, who, and how many times. Guys think if we get a woman drunk she'll say yes. Bull! She's already decided yes, getting drunk is a bonus.

— **Bob Dubac**

Men and women behave like our basic sexual elements. Single men on a weekend act like sperm: disorganized, bumping into each other, swimming in the wrong direction. "Let me through!" "You're on my tail!" They're the Three Billion Stooges. But the egg is cool, "Well, who's it going to be? I can divide. I can wait a month. I'm not swimming anywhere."

— **Jerry Seinfeld**

Women say they have sexual thoughts, too. They have no idea. It's the difference between shooting a bullet and throwing it. If they knew what we were really thinking, they'd never stop slapping us.

— **Larry Miller**

Men and women both care about smell, but women go to the trouble to smell good. Men are like, "Does this stink too bad to wear one more time? Maybe I should iron it."

— **Jeff Foxworthy**

Men always scratch their ass when they're thinking. Because that's where their brain is.

— **Tim Allen**

I was serving my country. It was either that, or six months.

— *Richard Pryor*

Being in the army is like being in the Boy Scouts, except that the Boy Scouts have adult supervision.

— *Blake Clark*

Why can't they have gay people in the army? Personally, I think they are just afraid of a thousand guys with M16s going, "Who'd you call a faggot?"

— *Jon Stewart*

I'd like to see gays in the military. If my wife will give me a night off now and then.

— *Dylan Brody*

I was thrown out of the Army for contributing to the delinquency of a major.

— *Strange de Jim*

* MONEY *

I don't like money, but it quiets my nerves.

— Joe E. Lewis

People say, "You should be able to be happy without money." Most of the people who say this have money. But there are times I can be happy without money. Like, during sex. But after sex, I like having a little money, and so does she.

— David Zasloff

I recently got one of those things where money is taken out of your paycheck before you get a chance to see it. What do you call that? Oh yeah, a wife.

— Peter Sasso

Money won't buy friends, but you get a better class of enemy.

— Spike Milligan

They say money talks. All it ever said to me was, "See ya, bitch."

— Rob Cantrell

There are more important things than money, but they won't date you if you don't have any.

— Henny Youngman

My brother is very wealthy now because he has one of those things, what do you call 'em? Oh yeah, a job. He goes every day, it's like he's obsessed.

— Gary Gulman

* MONOGAMY *

Monogamous sex is what one partner in every relationship wants it to be.

— Strange de Jim

A study shows that monogamous couples live longer. And cheaters who don't get caught live longer than cheaters who do.

— Jay Leno

It can take a man several marriages to understand the importance of monogamy.

— Jason Love

A man is only as faithful as his options.

— Chris Rock

* MOONING *

Here's a health warning: Don't moon a pit bull after sitting in A-1 sauce.

— Johnny Carson

Never moon a werewolf.

— Mike Binder

* MORNINGS *

Nothing good ever happens in the morning. Have you ever observed people in the morning? They tend to be flossing, scratching, or eating things like boiled eggs. At night, you drink fine wine and make love, neither of which requires flossing.

— Richard Jeni

My mother loved children. She would have given anything if I had been one.

— Groucho Marx

My parents were in a motorcycle gang. My mother used to breast-feed me on the back of a Harley Davidson doing 75 miles an hour. That's not right. She'd flip out a breast, it would be flopping around and by the time I got to the milk, it was butter. My mother also had nipple rings that weren't real gold, so I had a green mustache when I was finished.

— Dobie Maxwell

I have trouble telling women my feelings. I think it goes back to the first time I told my mom I loved her. I said, "I love you, Mommy." And she said, "Slow down, I'm not ready for that kind of commitment. You're going way too fast."

— Mike Rubin

I'm very loyal in a relationship, all relationships. When I'm with my mother, I don't look at other moms, "Wow. I wonder what her macaroni and cheese tastes like."

— Garry Shandling

I asked my mother if I was adopted. She said, "Not yet, but we placed an ad."

— Dana Snow

My mother never saw the irony in calling me a son-of-a-bitch.

— Richard Jeni

My mom was a little weird. When I was little mom would make chocolate frosting, and she'd let me lick the beaters. And then she'd turn them off.

— Marty Cohen

I was raised by just my mom. See, my father died when I was eight years old. At least, that's what he told us in the letter.

— Drew Carey

The relationship between mothers and children never changes and that's because no matter how rich or powerful you are your mother still remembers when you were three and put Spaghetti-Os up your nose.

— Dennis Miller

Dating is hard, and I figured out why. It's those damn romantic comedies. No guy can be this nice, sweet, and understanding. Here's a good example, my ex and I get out of a movie and she turns to me and asks, "Why can't you be more like those guys in the romantic comedies?" So I turned to her and said, "I don't know, why can't you be more like the chicks in pornos?"

— Todd Larson

So I go to the snack bar. I don't think it should be legal to call anything that costs $18.50 a snack. "Those Twizzlers look good, do you have financial aid?"

— David Spade

Movie Indians say, "White man speak with forked tongue." I wish! If I had a forked tongue I'd use it, I'd be scraping satisfied women off my bedroom ceiling with a spatula.

— Danny Liebert

* MOVING *

They say that moving is one of the most stressful things in life. Death in the family is the second most stressful and moving your dead spouse is the third.

— Kevin Nealon

* MUSIC *

In high school, I was in the marching band, so you know the babes were all over me.

— Drew Carey

I was listening to rap music this afternoon. Not that I had a choice, it was coming out of a Jeep four miles away.

— Nick DiPaulo

* NEIGHBORHOODS *

I grew up in the suburbs in a neighborhood that was not very tough at all. Even our school bully was only passively aggressive. He wouldn't take your lunch, he'd just say, "You're going to eat all that?"

— Brian Kiley

I tell ya, I come from a tough neighborhood. Why, just last week some guy pulled a knife on me. I could see it wasn't a real professional job. There was butter on it.

— Rodney Dangerfield

* NEWS *

Here's my thing with the news: I don't know what I'm supposed to do. By the time I read about something, it's obviously too late to help. If you told me that tomorrow a bus was going to go sailing off the Himalayas, I'd pick up the phone and warn them. "Don't get on the bus. Didn't you see the paper?"

— Paul Reiser

* NUDISTS *

This group is organizing the first airline flights for nudists. I don't even like the guy in the next seat touching me with his elbow. And Palm Springs is building the first nudist bridge. How'd you like to be the toll taker? "Hey, this quarter is warm!"

— Jay Leno

* OBITUARIES *

Roone Arledge died. He was most famous for inventing Monday Night Football, which revolutionized the way men ignore their wives.

— Craig Kilborn

How did Captain Hook die? He wiped with the wrong hand.

— Tommy Sledge

The founder of Reddi-Whip has died. For those younger readers, whipped cream was the dessert used for sex before apple pie.

— Jay Leno

The man who developed the SAT tests has died, when his car going 10 mph ran into a train going 60 mph.

— Craig Kilborn

* OBSCENITIES *

Some guy hit my fender, and I told him, "Be fruitful and multiply." But not in those words.

— Woody Allen

Someone shows me one of their fingers and I'm supposed to feel bad. I would feel worse if I got the toe, because it's not easy to give someone the toe. You've gotta get the shoe and sock off, get it up, "Look at that toe, buddy!" It would be really insulting to get the toe.

— Jerry Seinfeld

* OLYMPICS *

Women like curling. They get to see men pushing brooms.

— Jay Leno

My wife wants Olympic sex, once every four years.

— Rodney Dangerfield

Luge strategy? Lie flat and try not to die.

— Tim Steeves

So many events in the Olympics, I don't understand their connection to reality. Like in the Winter Olympics, the biathlon that combines cross-country skiing with shooting a gun. How many Alpine snipers are into this? To me, it's like combining swimming with strangling a guy.

— Jerry Seinfeld

If Curling is an Olympic sport, then oral sex is adultery. For that matter, oral sex should be an Olympic sport. I mean, it's harder to do than Curling. And, frankly, if you're good at it, you should get a medal.

— Lewis Black

Black folks are good at the Olympic sports you can learn to do free in the park. The white guy in track knows he's coming in last. He's just running for the jacket.

— D.L. Hughley

I went to the Olympics, but I could only get tickets for synchronized swimming. I hate to say this, but I prayed for one of them to get a cramp because, if I understand the rules correctly, if one of them drowns, they all have to.

— Anthony Clark

If they're making bowling an Olympic sport, why not drinking and driving, or waking up next to a fat girl?

— Dave Attell

* ORGASMS *

There are two types of female orgasm: real and fake. Men don't know which is which, because to men sex is like a car accident and determining the female orgasm is like being asked, "What did you see after the car went out of control?" "I heard a lot of screeching sounds. I was facing the wrong way at one point. And in the end my body was thrown clear."

— Jerry Seinfeld

Forty-six percent of women surveyed answered "Yes," when asked if they ever faked an orgasm. Actually they said, "Yes, yes! Oh God, yes!"

— Wayne Cotter

Women might be able to fake orgasms. But men can fake whole relationships.

— Jimmy Shubert

My ex-wife was multi-orgasmic. Married nine years, two orgasms. And I wasn't there for either of them, some guys at work told me about it.

— Ken Ferguson

Men can have multiple orgasms. It just takes us a week.

— **Tommy Koenig**

The only time my wife and I had a simultaneous orgasm was when the judge signed the divorce papers.

— **Woody Allen**

Boy, parents: there's a tough job. Damn easy job to get, though. I think most people love the interview. You don't have to dress for it.

— **Steve Bruner**

You wake up one day and say, "You know what, I don't think I ever need to sleep or have sex again." Congratulations, you're ready to have children.

— **Ray Romano**

How much being a parent would change my life didn't occur to me until I was heaving up my dinner the day my daughter was born.

— **Tim Allen**

Having children gives your life purpose. Right now my purpose is to get some sleep.

— **Reno Goodale**

You have a baby, you have to clean up your act. You can't come in drunk and go, "Hey, here's a little switch, Daddy's going to throw up on you."

— Robin Williams

Everyone should have kids. They are the greatest joy in the world. But they are also terrorists. You'll realize this as soon as they are born, and they start using sleep deprivation to break you.

— Ray Romano

A two-year old is like having a blender, but you don't have a top for it.

— Jerry Seinfeld

Sex after children slows down. Every three months now we have sex. Every time I have sex, the next day I pay my quarterly taxes. Unless it's oral sex — then I renew my driver's license.

— Ray Romano

It's a myth that you will be able to help your children with their homework. I'm taking remedial math so I can help my son make it to the third grade.

— **Sinbad**

I've got good kids, love my kids. I'm trying to bring them up the right way, not spanking them. I find waving the gun around gets the same job done.

— **Denis Leary**

Never raise your hands to your kids. It leaves your groin unprotected.

— **Red Buttons**

In a nutshell, just be good and kind to your children because not only are they the future of the world, they are the ones who can eventually sign you into the home.

— **Dennis Miller**

People have always told me that I'd learn more from my kids than they'd learn from me. I believe that. I've learned that as a parent, when you have sex your body emits a hormone that drifts down the hall into your child's room and makes them want a drink of water.

— **Jeff Foxworthy**

* PARENTS *

You don't ever really want to visualize your parents having sex. It's very uncomfortable. Sex is a great thing and all. But you don't want to think that your whole life began because somebody had a little too much wine with dinner.

— Jerry Seinfeld

I'll tell you when I first got the feeling my parents never wanted me. It was right after my fourth bris.

— Ed Bluestone

My parents used to take me to the pet department and tell me it was a zoo.

— Billy Connolly

Your parents are always giving you advice, "Never take money from strangers." So I used to take it out of her purse instead.

— George Wallace

My parents never felt I was good-looking. When they made home movies, they'd hire an actor to play me.

— Ed Bluestone

You finally get old enough to stay home alone when your parents go away on vacation, but they call back and ask stupid questions like, "How's the house?" I used to answer things like, "Oh, the house is sick. Yesterday it threw up all over the place."

— George Wallace

There are no perfect parents. Even Jesus had a distant father and a domineering mother. I'd have trust issues, if my father allowed me to be crucified.

— Bob Smith

People think living in your parents' basement until you're twenty-nine is lame. But what they don't realize is that while you're there, you save money on rent, food, and dates.

— Ray Romano

My parents' dream was for me to have everything they didn't. And thanks to ozone holes, fear of AIDS, and no health insurance, their dream has come true.

— Brad Slaight

When I went to college, my parents threw a going away party for me, according to the letter.

— Emo Philips

* PATRIOTISM *

If every man was as true to his country as he was to his wife, we'd be in a lot of trouble.

— Rodney Dangerfield

* PENISES *

The problem is that God gives men a brain and a penis, and only enough blood to run one at a time.

— Robin Williams

My penis is about ten inches long, if you include part of my large intestine.

— David Corrado

My theory is that women don't suffer from penis envy. Every man just thinks his penis is enviable. Maybe Freud suffered from Penis Doubt.

— Bob Smith

Women think men are led around by our penises. It points us in a direction, I'll give you that. But we're adult enough to make a decision whether to follow it. Granted, I put my back out trying to reel it back in.

— Garry Shandling

There's a product called Mr. Big Cream. Just rub it on your dick and it gets bigger. Well, if it worked, then wouldn't your hands get bigger, too?

— **Robert Schimmel**

Women say it's not how much men have, but what we do with it. How many things can we do with it? What is it, a Cuisinart? It's got two speeds: forward and reverse.

— **Richard Jeni**

* PHOBIAS *

My wife was afraid of the dark. Then she saw me naked. Now she's afraid of the light.

— **Rodney Dangerfield**

* PHONE SEX *

It kills me the way they advertise phone sex, "Phone up and hear a woman's secret fantasies." If there's any reality to this, you'd hear stuff like, "Yeah, I'd like to be paid the same as a man for the same job."

— **Mike MacDonald**

Some people have six-pack abs, I have a keg.

— *Craig Sharf*

I'm chunky. In a bathing suit I look like a Bartlett pear with a rubber band around it.

— *Drew Carey*

My doctor told me to exercise. He said walking would get me into shape. I said, "Doc, I've already chosen a shape, and it's round."

— *Irv Gilman*

* PORNOGRAPHY *

To men, pornos are beautiful love stories with all the boring stuff taken out.

— *Richard Jeni*

You know what I like more than women?
Pornography. Because I can get pornography.

— **Patton Oswalt**

I had to learn sex from porno movies. That doesn't
work. Learning sex from porno, that's like learning
how to drive by watching the Indianapolis 500.

— **Norman K.**

Every porno movie should be called "Stuff That
Never Happens to You."

— **Richard Jeni**

The State of California may soon regulate the porn
industry. What will that be like if the government
starts getting involved in sex? We'll have to have
mattresses with airbags, and we'll all have to wear
safety helmets to protect ourselves from hitting the
headboard. It will be a nightmare.

— **Jay Leno**

A Vermont woman caught her boyfriend watching
porn and shot him in the arm. Luckily it wasn't the
arm he uses for watching porn.

— **Conan O'Brien**

In Spain a 65-year-old man died watching a porno
movie and masturbating. All the guys at the funeral
were asking, "What channel was that?"

— **Jay Leno**

My girlfriend is at that stage where her biological clock is telling her it's time for her to be making me feel guilty and immature.

— Kevin Hench

Pregnancy is amazing. To think that you can create a human being just with the things you have around the house.

—Shang

On the reproductive front, researchers say the number one cause of pregnancy is sex. The number two cause is sex ten minutes later.

— Kevin Nealon

When I was growing up, the fertility drug was alcohol.

— Kelly Monteith

Doctor says to a man, "You're pregnant." The man asks, "How does a man get pregnant?" The doctor says, "The usual way: a little wine, a little dinner..."

— Henny Youngman

Natural childbirth class. A great place to find chicks, if you're into the full-figured gals. And you can be reasonably sure these girls put out.

— Jonathan Katz

* PREMATURE EJACULATION *

I went to a meeting for premature ejaculators. I left early.

— Red Buttons

My psychologist told me that a lot of men suffer from premature ejaculation. That's not true: women suffer.

— Robert Schimmel

* PREMENSTRUAL SYNDROME *

PMS is this very difficult hormonal syndrome that causes women, for four or five days out of every month, to behave exactly the way men do all the time.

— Dylan Brody

Science has found that men may suffer from PMS. Men suffer, too. The saddest part? I have my mother's thighs.

— Craig Kilborn

PRESIDENTS

So how do I pick a president? Much the same way I choose a driver to the airport. Which one will cost me the least, and not get me killed.

— Dennis Miller

I'd never run for president. I've thought about it, and the only reason I'm not is that I'm scared no woman would come forward and say she had sex with me.

— Garry Shandling

PRISONS

My friend Larry's in jail now. He got twenty-five years for something he didn't do. He didn't run fast enough.

— Damon Wayans

* PROSTITUTION *

I don't get no respect. I went to a massage parlor. It was self-service.

— Rodney Dangerfield

Hookers don't like to snuggle.

— Zach Galifiniakis

I don't respect prostitutes. I think they've sold out.

— Craig Sharf

You know what happens to a woman who is arrested for prostitution? She goes to jail. You know what happens to a man? He gets reelected.

— Jay Leno

* RACING *

I went to see a NASCAR race. Where did they get the name? Did two guys in North Carolina try to impress each other? "Hey Bubba, look at mah new Chevrolet." "WHOOOEEEE, Nahhhhsssss Car."

— Dobie Maxwell

I watched the Indy 500. And I was thinking: if they left earlier, they wouldn't have to go so fast.

— Steven Wright

* RELATIONSHIPS *

The difference between being in a relationship and being in prison is that in prison they let you play softball on the weekends.

— Bobby Kelton

Relationships are a lot like drugs. You develop a dependency, and if you're not really careful you could wind up losing your house.

— Mike Dugan

I deserve someone who likes me for who I am pretending to be.

— Arj Barker

Honesty is the key to a relationship. If you can fake that, you're in.

— Rich Jeni

When I'm not in a relationship, I shave one leg. So when I sleep, it feels like I'm with a woman.

— Garry Shandling

Relationships are hard. It's like a full-time job, and we should treat it like one. If your boyfriend or girlfriend wants to leave you, they should give you two weeks' notice. There should be severance pay, and before they leave you, they have to find you a temp.

— Bob Ettinger

* REMOTE CONTROLS *

I want one more remote control unit in my life. I want twelve of those suckers lined up on the coffee table, bring the friends over and go, "See those? I don't know how to work any of them. Zero for twelve."

— Paul Reiser

I couldn't find the remote control to the remote control.

— Steven Wright

A new survey reveals that women would rather give up sex than give up the remote for the TV. Men, on the other hand, would be willing to have sex *with* the remote for the TV.

— Conan O'Brien

* RESTAURANTS *

I was at a fancy restaurant. They had a waiter for everything. The butter waiter came over and gave us butter, the water waiter came over and gave us water, the head waiter came over . . . oh, it was so fancy.

— George Miller

If you're a guy and you ask for the doggie bag on a date, you might as well have them wrap up your genitals, too. You're not going to be needing those for a while, either.

— Jerry Seinfeld

I once dated a waitress. In the middle of sex she'd say, "How is everything? Is everything okay over here?"

— David Corrado

Have you ever been in a restaurant and a couple in the next booth is being overly affectionate? They're necking and groping and you're trying to eat your eggs. I always want to go up to them and say, "Excuse me, mind if I join you?" What are these people thinking? Do they wake up in the morning and ask each other, "Want to have sex, honey?" "No, let's wait until we get to Denny's."

— Bobby Kelton

* ROMANCE *

Fifty percent of the American population spends less than ten dollars a month on romance. You know what we call these people? Men.

— Jay Leno

What is my favorite romantic spot? You mean in the whole world or on somebody's body?

— Jackie Mason

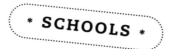

* SCHOOLS *

I will never forget my first day of school. My mom woke me up, got me dressed, made my bed and fed me. Man, did the guys in the dorm tease me.

— Michael Aronin

My kindergarten teacher hated me. She used to find any excuse to pick on me, especially during nap time. Like I'm the only guy who sleeps naked.

— **Brian Kiley**

A lot of stuff in school you don't appreciate 'til you get to be older. Little things, like being spanked everyday by a middle-aged woman. Stuff you'd pay good money for later in life.

— **Emo Philips**

The gym teacher Mr. Caruso did not speak English; he spoke "Gym." One day I was playing basketball and Mr. Caruso told me to get an athletic supporter. He didn't say it that way, though. He said, "One day you're gonna go up for a rebound and the family jewels aren't gonna go with ya." I had no idea what he was talking about. Next day I showed up for practice without my watch and mezuzah. He said, "Did ya take care of the family jewels?" I said, "I left 'em in my locker." Took us a half hour to revive Mr. Caruso.

— **Gabe Kaplan**

My school colors were clear. We used to say, "I'm not naked, I'm in the band."

— **Steven Wright**

There's always one teacher you had a crush on. For me it's my wife's aerobics instructor.

— Brian Kiley

I remember my prom, the limo, the dancing until dawn. It would have been even better if I'd had a date.

— David Letterman

I was home-schooled. The cat never stood a chance against me in dodge ball.

— Eric Roth

Don't go to your high school reunion. You know who goes to your high school reunion? Idiots. Everybody you hated in high school shows up. The really cool people overdosed years ago, or they're living elsewhere under the witness protection program.

— Billy Garan

* SCOUTING *

The only memory I have of being a Cub Scout was trying to get my hat back. That was all I did. Run back and forth at my bus stop going, "Quit it!"

— Jerry Seinfeld

When I was in Boy Scouts, I slipped on the ice and hurt my ankle. A little old lady had to help me across the street.

— Steven Wright

* SELF-CONSCIOUSNESS *

I was so self-conscious that when I was at a football game and the players went into a huddle — I thought they were talking about me.

— Jackie Mason

* SELF-ESTEEM *

I'm currently dating a girl with no self-esteem. Which is good, because if she had any, she'd leave me.

— Devin Dugan

I have low self-esteem. When we were in bed together, I would fantasize that I was someone else.

— Richard Lewis

* SEX *

According to *Psychology Today*, to keep your sex life active as a married couple, you should engage in role-playing. This works. Once a month my wife and I check into a cheap motel, and she pretends to be a hooker while I pretend to be a TV evangelist.

— Wally Wang

I actually learned about sex watching neighborhood dogs. And it was good. Go ahead and laugh. I think the most important thing I learned was: never let go of the girl's leg no matter how hard she tries to shake you off.

— Steve Martin

My problems all boil down to how I learned about sex. When I was little I asked my father, "What's a vagina?" He said, "It's an aerial view of geese." But then I asked, "What's a clitoris? Everyone's talking about it." My dad said, "It's a mouthwash." So I've spent the rest of my life looking for three women who, by chance, happen to be walking in formation while gargling.

— Richard Lewis

Sex is simple, once you realize it's just like riding a bicycle. In both cases, the hardest part is learning not to fall off.

— Strange de Jim

In sex-ed classes in Great Britain they're actually recommending oral sex as a way to cut down on unwanted pregnancies. It's the first time even the stupid kids are telling the teacher at the end of class, "You forgot to give us our assignment!"

— Jay Leno

Is sex dirty? Only if it's done right.

— Woody Allen

When my teenage daughter told us that her sex-ed teacher had demonstrated how to put on a condom, my wife asked, "On what? A cucumber? Boy, are they letting you in for a big disappointment."

— Robert Schimmel

I'm not a good lover, but at least I'm fast.

— Drew Carey

I asked my wife to try anal sex. She said, "Sure. You first."

— Robert Schimmel

Back in high school, my buddies tried to put the make on anything that moved. I told them, "Why limit yourselves?"

— Emo Philips

I'm not good in bed. Hell, I'm not even good on the couch.

— **Drew Carey**

I think sex is beautiful between the right man and the right woman, but it's difficult to get between the right man and woman.

— **Woody Allen**

Casual sex is the best, because you don't have to wear a tie.

— **John Mendoza**

I never believed in casual sex. I have always tried as hard as I could.

— **Garry Shandling**

I'm in kind of a sexual dry spell. For the past few years, I've only had sex in the months that end in "arch."

— **Doug Benson**

My love life is terrible. The last time I was inside a woman was when I visited the Statue of Liberty.

— **Woody Allen**

A study in a magazine asked men, "Would you rather the woman initiate sex?" Overwhelmingly, men said "Yes!" Women countered with the argument saying,

"But every time we do we get rejected and criticized."
Welcome to the club.

— **Jack Coen**

No matter what she says or does, remember one
thing — all women want it. But maybe not with you.

— **Bill Kalmenson**

I once made love to a female clown, and she twisted
my penis into a poodle.

— **Dan Whitney**

I tell ya, I got no sex life. My dog watched me in the
bedroom, to learn how to beg. He also taught my
wife how to roll over and play dead.

— **Rodney Dangerfield**

My wife told me of a book about the G-Spot. I went
to a bookstore, I couldn't even find the book. My
wife bought it for me, but there were no pictures,
maps, or diagrams. It just said the G-spot was about
two-thirds of the way in. Compared to who?

— **Robert Schimmel**

Sex after a fight is often the best there is, which is
why you're never allowed in the locker room right
after a prizefight.

— **Jay Leno**

There's a lot of pressure on men to find that G-spot.
I've got trouble enough just finding a parking spot,
how am I gonna find something I can't see?

— Tommy Koenig

In a new sex survey they found eight percent of people had sex four or more times a week. Now here's the interesting part. That number drops to two percent when you add the phrase, "With partner."

— David Letterman

After making love I said to my girl, "Was it good for you, too?" And she said, "I don't think that was good for anybody."

— Garry Shandling

I tried group sex. Now I have a new problem. I don't know who to thank.

— Rodney Dangerfield

Having sex is like playing bridge. If you don't have a good partner, you better have a good hand.

— **Woody Allen**

In Germany, police are searching for a woman who holds men at gunpoint and forces them to have sex with her. Actually the gun isn't for the sex, it's to keep the guy around later to make him cuddle.

— **Jay Leno**

People in different parts of the world react differently after sex. A German woman is practical. She will say, "Ach, dat vas goot!" A French woman is solicitous. She will say, "Ah, mon cherie, did I please you?" and an English woman will say, "Feeling better?"

— **Godfrey Cambridge**

The other night I was making love to my wife, and she said, "Deeper, deeper." So I started quoting Nietzsche to her.

— **Dennis Miller**

I read in *Cosmopolitan* that women like to have whipped cream sprayed on their breasts. Unfortunately, my girlfriend has silicone implants. So I use non-dairy topping.

— **Jeff Shaw**

My girlfriend always laughs during sex, no matter what she's reading.

— *Emo Philips*

My wife insists on turning off the lights when we make love. That doesn't bother me. It's the hiding that seems so cruel.

— *Jonathan Katz*

Sex without love is an empty experience, but as empty experiences go it's one of the best.

— *Woody Allen*

Everybody lies about sex. People lie during sex. If it weren't for lies, there'd be no sex.

— *Jerry Seinfeld*

Ménage à trois is a French term. It means Kodak moment.

— *Greg Ray*

It seems like we hear more talk about the threesome in sex. And when I was single that was sincerely never a fantasy of mine. It was never like, "How could I wake up with two disappointed ladies tomorrow?"

— *Bob Goldthwait*

Women need a reason to have sex. Men just need a place.

— **Billy Crystal**

The basic conflict between men and women sexually, is that men are like firemen. To us, sex is an emergency, and no matter what we're doing we can be ready in two minutes. Women are like fire. They're very exciting, but the conditions have to be exactly right for it to occur.

— **Jerry Seinfeld**

I have tried a little kinky stuff. A woman called me and said, "I have mirrors all over my bedroom. Bring a bottle." I brought Windex.

— **Rodney Dangerfield**

Men love oral sex because it combines the two activities that the average guy never gets tired of: 1. Sex 2. Not moving at all. If the Superbowl was on I could die right now.

— **Richard Jeni**

Don't have sex, man. It leads to kissing, and pretty soon you have to start talking to them.

— **Steve Martin**

The first time I ever got undressed in front of a woman, it was horrible. She started screaming, and then they kicked me off the bus.

— James Leemer

If you have sex and you know you've made the other person happy, it's so much better than doing it for yourself. Although if you're using your left hand, it's really like you're doing it with someone else.

— Jim Carrey

I've had more women than most people have noses.

— Steve Martin

I told my girlfriend that unless she expressed her feelings and told me what she liked, I wouldn't be able to please her. So she said, "Get off me."

— Garry Shandling

When my wife has sex with me there's always a reason. One night she used me to time an egg.

— Rodney Dangerfield

The newlyweds were married five days. He turns to her and says, "Honey, we're gonna make love a new way tonight. We're gonna lie back to back." She says, "How can that be any fun?" He says, "I've invited another couple."

— Woody Woodbury

I'm not into that one-night thing. I think a person should get to know someone, and even be in love with them, before you use them and degrade them.

— Steve Martin

Into bondage? I am. What I do when I'm in the mood is tie her up, and gag her, and go into the living room and watch football.

— Tom Arnold

I bet the Marquis de Sade would have liked the Three Stooges.

— David Corrado

I practice safe sex. Some day I'd like to perform it.

— Adam Richmond

I practice safe sex. I use an airbag. It's a little startling at first when it flies out. Then the woman realizes it's safer than being thrown clear.

— Garry Shandling

During sex my wife always wants to talk to me. Just the other night she called me from a hotel.

— Rodney Dangerfield

I once made love for an hour and five minutes. It was on the day they push the clock ahead.

— Garry Shandling

I had sex for five hours once, but four and a half was apologizing.

— Conan O'Brien

There's now bubble gum with Viagra. It gets very big and then pops.

— Craig Kilborn

I don't need Viagra. I need a pill to help me talk afterwards.

— Garry Shandling

In a survey for *Modern Maturity* magazine, men over 75 said they had sex once a week. Which proves that old guys lie about sex, too.

— Irv Gilman

In Italy an 85-year-old man and a 75-year-old woman were arrested for having sex in a parked car, and the left-turn signal was on the whole time.

— Jay Leno

I once saw my grandparents have sex, and that's why I don't eat raisins.

— Zach Galifiniakis

Republicans are upset that federal funds are being used by the Kinsey Institute to study sexual arousal. Republicans are against using federal funds to study sexual arousal unless the study leads to impeachment.

— Jay Leno

* SHOPPING *

Here's how a guy shops. He's standing outside. He goes, "I'm cold." He goes in the store, buys the coat, walks out, "I'm not cold anymore. Shopping is over."

— Ritch Shydner

Beverly Hills requires that stores put this label on all fur coats: "Warning: Your husband is having an affair."

— Craig Kilborn

Women try on clothes different from men. They hold a dress up against themselves, stick one leg out, because they need to know, "What if someday I'm one-legged, and at a forty-five degree angle?" A guy never takes a suit off the rack, puts his head in the neck, and asks, "What do you think? Put some shoes by the bottom of the pants. What if I'm walking? Move the shoes."

— Jerry Seinfeld

* SINGLE LIFE *

Married or single? I have to compare the disadvantages of each: marriage or not? Do I wanna go out every night talking about a bunch of stuff I'm not really interested in just to see if I can get some sex out of it? Or, do I wanna be married talking about a bunch of stuff I've heard before just to see if I can get some sex out of it?

— Richard Jeni

I'm single by choice. Not my choice.

— Orny Adams

It's pretty lonely and sad to be single. Every night was the same for me, I'd go home and curl up in bed with my favorite book. Well, actually it was a magazine.

— Tom Arnold

I got married to complicate my thought process. When you're single, your brain is single-minded. Single guys think three things: "I'd like to go out with her," "I'd like to buy one of those," and "I hope those guys win."

— Jerry Seinfeld

* SKIING *

Cross-country skiing is great if you live in a small country.

— Steven Wright

I pay approximately $1,300 for a lift ticket which makes me eligible for the lift chair. I don't know who invented this death machine. This is like a psycho's physics test with benches whipping by. Suddenly you're inside a math word problem. "Estimate the velocity of a bench . . ." Great, the one day I forgot my protractor.

— Wayne Federman

I say, why pay outrageous prices for ski trips, when I can just stick my face in the freezer and fall down on the kitchen floor?

— John Wagner

* SLEEPING *

If I'm not in bed by eleven at night, I go home.

— Henny Youngman

I never get enough sleep. I stay up late because I'm a Night Guy. "What about getting up after five hours sleep?" "That's Morning Guy's problem." So you get up in the morning, you're exhausted. Night Guy screws Morning Guy. The only thing Morning Guy can do is oversleep enough so Day Guy loses his job and Night Guy has no money to go out.

— Jerry Seinfeld

Women like to spoon in bed, whereas men just like to fork.

— Jason Love

Married men, want to drive your wife crazy? When you go home, don't talk in your sleep: just grin.

— Henny Youngman

* SMOKING *

My lady friend wants me to give up cigars. I don't want to. So we compromised. I will only smoke on nights that I'm with other women.

— Craig Kilborn

They say that kissing a smoker is like licking an ash tray — which is a good thing to remember the next time you get lonely.

— Fred Stoller

I don't let men smoke in my apartment. But if I have a woman over she can barbecue a goat.

— Todd Barry

You know what bugs me? People who smoke cigars in restaurants. That's why I always carry a water pistol filled with gasoline.

— Paul Provenza

* SPERM *

People make a living donating to sperm banks. Last year I let five hundred dollars slip through my fingers.

— Robert Schimmel

I have nothing against sperm banks, but they should really get rid of those automatic teller machines.

— David Corrado

My personal history: I started out as a sperm. Good swimmer. Liked eggs. Nine months, mom kicks me out of my first home. Since then, I've been living on the outside and looking for similar accommodations. I find them occasionally, but I make a mess and have to leave.

— Basil White

A man can produce sperm until he dies. But at least it's more fun than getting killed crossing the street.

— Strange de Jim

* SPORTS *

I used to be quite an athlete, big chest, hard stomach. But all that's behind me now.

— Bob Hope

I bought a newspaper the other day and I was gonna flip to the sports section when I realized, I just don't want to read about vicious brawls, random drug testing, salary squabbles, or venomous court proceedings. For chrissakes, it's enough to make you wanna go to the front page.

— **Dennis Miller**

We're a little too into sports in this country, I think we gotta throttle back. People come home from these games, "We won! We won!" No, they won: you watched.

— **Jerry Seinfeld**

I used to compete in sports, and then I realized: you can buy trophies. Now I'm good at everything.

— **Demetri Martin**

Women play for the reason male athletes used to play: the love of the game. When I read about male professional athletes being arrested for murder, assault, rape, and theft, I agree with those who say they just can't see women competing on the same level as men anytime in the near future.

— **Dennis Miller**

I tried bungee jumping. They don't tell you to take the change out of your pockets.

— **Tony DePaul**

If you're not into sports, guys think you're less of a man unless you can account for time in activities equally masculine. When they ask, "Wanna go see the game?" I reply, "I can't. I gotta go put a transmission in a stripper's car."

— **Bob Nickman**

Can't we silence those Christian athletes who thank Jesus whenever they win, and never mention His name when they lose? You never hear them say, "Jesus made me drop the ball," "The good Lord tripped me up behind the line of scrimmage."

— **George Carlin**

Victory goes to the player who makes the next-to-last mistake.

— **Jackie Mason**

The world's best darts player has died at 66. Cause of death was the world's worst darts player.

— **Craig Kilborn**

My neighborhood is so bad I started taking karate lessons. I learned how to break my hand in half by hitting a brick.

— **David Corrado**

I was ejected from a skating rink today. Evidently they don't allow ice fishing.

— Kevin Nealon

An assault in hockey, or as they call it in the 'hood, white-on-white crime.

— Jay Leno

Some people play a horse to win, some to place. I should have bet this horse to live.

— Henny Youngman

Scuba-diving. A great activity where your main goal is, Just Don't Die.

— Jerry Seinfeld

I was skydiving, horizontally.

— Steven Wright

I went snow boarding today. Well actually, I went careening off a mountain on a giant tongue depressor.

— Paul Provenza

I play tennis, and I'm pretty good, but no matter how much I practice I'll never be as good as a wall.

— **Mitch Hedberg**

I'd lift weights, but they're so damn heavy.

— **Jason Love**

Today in America, a professional wrestler is struck down with a folding chair once every thirty-five seconds. And not one is seen by a referee.

— **Bill Maher**

* STRIPPERS *

Strippers are supposed to be a real macho thing to go see. I never understood this. Who was the first guy who wanted this? Somebody sitting around reading Playboy? "This isn't frustrating enough, I'd like to see some live chicks I can't have."

— **Bob Nickman**

Strippers don't like it when you tip them in quarters.

— **Bil Dwyer**

In West Virginia a guy stole $500,000 from a truck parked outside a strip show. Police are questioning a man who's in his third day of a lap dance.

— **Craig Kilborn**

If you go to a strip club when you told your wife or girlfriend you were going out to paint churches or something, here's my advice: don't get the stripper wearing the glitter. It will seem like a good idea at the time, but you'll be going home covered in stripper dust, and that's a tough one to get out of. "What are you doing with all that glitter on you?" "Making you a card."

— **John Heffron**

Utah is considering a tax on topless dancers. Luckily there's no flat tax.

— **Jay Leno**

According to *USA Today*, physicist Steven Hawking visited a strip club. At the club he commented, "The universe isn't the only thing that's expanding."

— **Conan O'Brien**

I went to a strip club, totally nude. Sure, my testicles stuck to the chair . . .

— **Bil Dwyer**

* SWIMMING *

Swimming isn't a sport. It's just a way to keep from drowning. Riding a bus isn't a sport; so why should sailing be a sport?

— **George Carlin**

I can't swim, but I don't consider myself a failure. Instead, I like to think I'm fully evolved.

— **Brian Beatty**

I discovered I scream the same way whether I'm about to be devoured by a Great White, or if a piece of seaweed touches my foot.

— **Kevin James**

If you see a shark, you don't have to swim faster than the shark. You only have to swim faster than the person you're with.

— **Kevin Nealon**

* TALKING *

Women will gab at each other for fifty-seven hours, breaking down every emotional thing they're going through into nuances. A man will sit down with his buddy and his buddy will ask, "What's up with your wife?" The man will mumble, "Oh, man, she's tripping." End of analysis.

— Sinbad

I haven't talked to my wife in three weeks. I don't want to interrupt her.

— Henny Youngman

The other night in bed my wife was saying sexy things. I looked up, and she was on the phone.

— Rodney Dangerfield

I hate it when a woman says, "Talk dirty to me." I want to ask, "Can't I just give you the finger?"

— Tommy Koenig

I talk to my wife while making love, if I happen to be near a phone.

— Henny Youngman

* TATTOOS *

I always look for a woman who has a tattoo. I see a woman with a tattoo and I'm thinking, "Okay, here's a gal who's capable of making a decision she'll regret in the future."

— Richard Jeni

* TAXATION *

The IRS, they're like the Mafia, they can take anything they want.

— Jerry Seinfeld

How many people use the E-Z tax filing form? Actually they don't call it that anymore. It's now titled, "Okay, go ahead and screw me, I can't find my receipts."

— Jay Leno

While no one likes paying taxes, we should all remember what our taxes pay for: blowing people up.

— Craig Kilborn

I don't like the idea that people can call you in your car. I think there's news you shouldn't get at sixty miles per hour. "Pregnant? Whoaah!"

— Tom Parks

Cordless phones are great. If you can find them.

— Glen Foster

If I had a vibrating pager, I would get a mobile phone and call myself. Stand around hitting re-dial all day.

— Dan Wilson

There's now a cell phone that's also a vibrator. How many car accidents will that thing cause? You no longer have to let your fingers do the walking.

— Jay Leno

The government has new regulations for telemarketers. Even better, the government told the telemarketers by calling them during dinner.

— Conan O'Brien

I called the Injury Hotline and told them I was hurting for cash.

— Jay London

* TELEVISION *

Men flip around the television more than women. Men get that remote control, don't know what the hell they're watching, just keep going, "Rerun, that's stupid, he's stupid, *go, go, go!*" "I think it's a documentary about your father." "Don't care, what else is on?" Women will stop and go, "Let's see what the show is, before I change the channel. Maybe we work with it, help it grow into something." Because women nest, and men hunt: that's why we watch TV differently.

— Jerry Seinfeld

I watch the Discovery Channel and you know what I've discovered? I need a girlfriend. The more Discovery Channel you watch, the less chance you ever have of meeting a woman, because it fills your head full of odd facts that can come out at any moment, "Hello. Did you know Hitler was ticklish? That the sea otter has four nipples? Don't run away!"

— Dave Attell

The cable TV sex channels don't expand our horizons, don't make us better people, and don't come in clearly enough.

— Bill Maher

I got 24-hour porn on my satellite, so I don't come out of my house for too many reasons. I've got to go home soon because another one is starting, and I don't want to miss the beginning. If you miss the beginning of a dirty flick you can't follow the rest of the movie.

— Richard Jeni

Anti-violence advocates contend that violence on TV is directly linked to the rise of violence in society and officials are doing nothing about it. They pointed out that even some cartoons such as the Road Runner are violent, resulting in a proposed bill calling for a mandatory five-day waiting period before the purchase of an anvil, or any ACME product including TNT detonators and strap-on rockets.

— Kevin Nealon

* TOOLS *

A guy's in his driveway working with tools, all the men in the neighborhood are magnetically drawn to this. Men hear a drill, it's like a dog whistle. That's why construction sites have fences with holes so we can see what's going on, because if they didn't, we are climbing those fences. "Are you using steel girders? Yeah, that'll hold."

— Jerry Seinfeld

A man's not a man until he can find his way to Sears blindfolded, and the Craftsman tool department makes his nipples rock hard.

— **Tim Allen**

* TRANSSEXUALS *

San Francisco is going to pay for city employees who want sex changes. The city will save money, though. After they change a man to a woman, they only have to pay her seventy-five percent of what he was making. The HMO version is a sock to stuff down your pants, and a remote control. "OK, you're a guy."

— **Jay Leno**

Last year my friend George and I drove across the country. We switched on the driving, every half-mile. We had one tape to listen to the entire trip. I don't remember what it was.

— Steven Wright

I just got back from a pleasure trip. I drove my mother-in-law to the airport.

— Henny Youngman

* UGLINESS *

I'm so ugly, as a kid, I once stuck my head out the window and got arrested for mooning.

— Rodney Dangerfield

* UNDERWEAR *

Push-up bras are like breasts on the half-shell.

— **Dom Irrerra**

In Arkansas police arrested a man who'd broken into 14 homes and stolen nothing but women's panties. The panties were all returned to their rightful owner, Tom Jones.

— **Craig Kilborn**

You know what I say about edible panties? I say if you're drunk enough, and your teeth are sharp enough, every panty is edible.

— **Brian McKim**

I got some new underwear the other day. Well, new to me.

— **Emo Philips**

Two guys in a health club, one is putting on pantyhose. "Since when do you wear pantyhose?" one asks. "Since my wife found them in the glove compartment of my car."

— **Henny Youngman**

* WARS *

If women ran the world we wouldn't have wars. Just intense negotiations every 28 days.

— *Robin Williams*

* WEAPONRY *

The very existence of flame throwers proves that some time, somewhere, someone said to themselves, "You know, I want to set those people over there on fire, but I'm just not close enough to get the job done."

— *George Carlin*

* WEATHER *

It was so cold that I haven't got such a chill up my spine since I heard the words, "Honey, I'm pregnant."

— *David Letterman*

How hot is it? It's so hot that I saw two palm trees fighting over a dog.

— Rick Rockwell

* WEDDINGS *

If the wedding invitations were left up to the men, we'd drive around sticking flyers in windshields. Not even typed up either, just Magic Marker, Xeroxed, "Party!"

— Jerry Seinfeld

A man is suing a strip club for serious injuries suffered at his bachelor party when the girls jumped on him. He couldn't consummate his marriage the next night. Yeah, because his wife jumped all over him when she found out about the strippers.

— Jay Leno

It was one of those bachelor parties where all the married men had to meet at the end and decide about what to say we did, "We got in a fight with some guys and that's how our underwear got ripped. They ripped our underwear, and smelled good. Jimmy, you fell and your nipple got pierced."

— Ray Romano

I'm afraid of commitment. I'd get married if they'd reverse the vow: "Do I?"

— Al Lubel

I was the best man at a wedding. I thought the title was a bit much. If I'm the best man, why is she marrying him?

— Jerry Seinfeld

It seems like the only times they pronounce you anything in life is when they pronounce you man and wife, or dead on arrival.

— Dennis Miller

What are the scariest words known to man? "Till death do us part. Why not, "Until my car breaks down?" Or "Until I run out of money?"

— Damon Wayans

My wedding day, that was a beauty. I went to put the ring on, she gave me the wrong finger.

— **Rodney Dangerfield**

I wanted to look good for my wedding pictures. You might be looking at those things for four or five years.

— **Tom Arnold**

In Jamaica, forty couples were joined in a nude wedding. That's every young girl's dream, isn't it, being given away by her nude dad?

— **David Letterman**

You know what the best part of getting married is? Opening the envelopes. That way you get to see how cheap your relatives really are.

— **Joey Callahan**

Honeymoon night was hot. She was moaning all night in ecstasy, opening gifts. "An orange squeezer! Oh my God! A waffle maker!" Next morning the guy down the hall gave me the big thumbs-up. "Boy, you were using everything but the kitchen sink in there."

— **Mike Binder**

* WEIGHT *

My favorite health club is the International House of Pancakes. Because no matter what you weigh, there will always be someone who weighs 150 pounds more than you.

— Lewis Black

You know you're getting fat when you can pinch an inch on your forehead.

— John Mendoza

* WILLS *

My wife finally convinced me to sign what's called a living will. It's a document which gives her the right, if I become attached to some mechanical device, to terminate my life. So, yesterday, I'm on the exercise bike . . .

— Jonathan Katz

WINE

I've been making wine at home, but I'm making it out of raisins so it will be aged automatically.

— Steven Wright

WIVES

My wife made me get glasses. I wasn't seeing things her way.

— Mark Klein

My wife is the sweetest, most tolerant, most beautiful woman in the world. This is a paid political announcement.

— Henny Youngman

Any husband who says, "My wife and I are completely equal partners," is talking about either a law firm or a hand of bridge.

— Bill Cosby

In my house I'm the boss, my wife is just the decision maker.

— Woody Allen

Two guys meet on the street. "Hi, Charley," greeted one, "How's your wife?" "Compared to what?" responded the other.

— **Henny Youngman**

A good wife always forgives her husband when she's wrong.

— **Milton Berle**

Living with my wife is like taking orders from a drill sergeant. I have to work damn hard to go for a weekend pass.

— **Irv Gilman**

I met my wife in a bar. What a surprise, I thought she was home watching the kids.

— **Ron Dentinger**

With my wife I don't get no respect. The other night she told me to take out the garbage. I told her I already took out the garbage. Then she told me to go out and keep an eye on it.

— **Rodney Dangerfield**

My wife wants me to be sensitive, discuss my feelings and buy flowers. She wants me to be a girl, basically.

— Reno Goodale

My wife thinks I'm too nosy. At least that's what she keeps scribbling in her diary.

— Drake Sather

With my wife, I gave up. The other night, I told her, "You win, you're the boss. When it comes to sex, it'll be in your hands." She said, "You're wrong, it'll be in your hands."

— Rodney Dangerfield

In bed my wife sprawls out all over the mattress. I said, "I'm tired of only having two inches in this bed." She said "Now you know how I feel."

— Peter Sasso

With my wife nothing comes easy. When I want sex she leaves the room to give me privacy.

— Rodney Dangerfield

Sexually, my wife is very responsive. The trouble is, her response is always, "No."

— Reno Goodale

I tell ya, my wife likes to talk during sex. The other night she called me from a motel.

— **Rodney Dangerfield**

My wife wanted to go someplace expensive over the weekend, so I took her to a Shell station.

— **Jay Leno**

I take my wife everywhere, but she always finds her way home.

— **Henny Youngman**

My ex-wife, what was her name again? Oh yeah, Plaintiff.

— **David Letterman**

It's spicier having sex with your ex-wife isn't it? It's like you're cheating on yourself.

— **Tom Arnold**

Women are more verbal than men. That's why when you see an elderly couple together, it's always the man who has the hearing aid.

— **Jeff Stilson**

My ex-wife and I had the same problem: we couldn't stop thinking of her.

— **Jason Love**

* WOMEN *

Anyone who says he can see through women is missing a lot.

— Groucho Marx

I can't figure women out. They put on makeup for three hours. They wear things that make them smaller. Things that make them bigger. Then they meet a man and they want truth.

— Rodney Dangerfield

Women are the most powerful magnet in the universe. All men are cheap metal. And we know where north is.

— Larry Miller

If man could create the perfect woman, he'd probably cheat on her.

— **Jason Love**

Like most men, I want a woman who is a slut in the bedroom and a master chef in the kitchen. But I'm willing to compromise, I don't have to eat.

— **Tommy Koenig**

Do we know much about women? Do we? We don't. We know when they're happy, we know when they're crying, we know when they're pissed off. We just don't know what order those are going to come at us.

— **Evan Davis**

Could any man ever learn that mystical thing called a woman's intuition? Which isn't mystical at all, but rather an ability to pick up and process subtle clues that men lack because we're kind of dense.

— **Bill Cosby**

Women cannot complain about men anymore until they start getting better taste in them.

— **Bill Maher**

When a man says "fine," he means everything's fine. When a woman says "fine" she means, "I'm really ticked off, and you have to find out why."

— John Rogers

Women now have choices. They can be married, not married, have a job, not have a job, be married with children, unmarried with children. Men have the same choice we've always had: work or prison.

— Tim Allen

Women want food, water, and compliments. Know what men want? Food, sex, and silence.

— Chris Rock

According to women's magazines, men are losing the battle of the sexes. Women are raising their own children. They got their own careers. A couple of D-cell batteries and *boom*! we're outta there.

— Jack Coen

A study in the Washington Post says that women have better verbal skills than men. I just want to say to the authors of that study: duh.

— Conan O'Brien

Women. You can't live with them, and you can't get them to dress up in a skimpy Nazi costume and beat you with a warm squash.

— Emo Philips

Women need to like the job of the guy they're with. Men, if they are physically attracted to a woman, are not that concerned with her job. "Slaughterhouse? You're just lopping their heads off? Great! Why don't you shower, and we'll get some burgers."

— Jerry Seinfeld

* ZOOS *

Zoos are starting to give contraceptives to their animals. I can barely open a condom, and I have thumbs.

— Craig Kilborn

When I was a kid I got no respect. My old man took me to the zoo. He told me to go over to the leopard and play connect the dots.

— Rodney Dangerfield

The San Francisco Zoo had its annual Valentine's Day sex tour. They said bears would rather masturbate than have sex. That's why they get so mad when hikers surprise them. And when they break into campsites, they're not looking for food. They're looking for magazines.

— Jay Leno

* GREEN ROOM *

Veteran funnyman **Joey Adams,** a syndicated comedy columnist, was also the author of 23 humor books and hosted various radio and television programs.

*

Comedian **Max Alexander** has been the opening act for singer Tom Jones and was featured in the movies *Punchline* and *Roxanne.*

*

Comedian **Paul Alexander** has appeared on Comedy Central's *Comedy Product* and HBO's *Mr. Show.*

*

Comedian **Tim Allen** has been the star of the now-syndicated sitcom *Home Improvement* and movies that include *Toy Story* and *Galaxy Quest.*

*

Woody Allen is a comedian, actor, and Academy Award-winning director of films that include *Annie Hall* and *Mighty Aphrodite.*

*

Comedian **Jeff Altman** appears regularly on *The Late Show with David Letterman,* has guest-starred in dozens of network prime-time shows, including *Caroline in the City*, *Land's End,* and *Baywatch*, and his film credits include *Highlander II*, *American Hot Wax*, *Soul Man,* and *Easy Money.*

*

Musical comedian **Steve Altman** uses a sampling keyboard as his "gateway to madness." His television credits include A&E's *Evening at the Improv*, Showtime's *Comedy Club Network*, Caroline's *Comedy Hour*, MTV, VH1, Fox's *Comic Strip Live,* and HBO.

*

Morey Amsterdam was a comedian best known for his role as a comedy writer on *The Dick Van Dyke Show*.

*

Jack Archey is a CPA who decided that having a steady, well-paying job was drastically overrated, and has since performed his comedy at the Comedy Store, the LA Comedy Cabaret, and the Hollywood Laugh Factory.

*

Tom Arnold is a comedian and actor who has appeared in the movies *True Lies* and *Nine Months*.

*

Michael Aronin is a stand-up comedian and an accomplished motivational speaker. Website: www.michaelaronin.com.

Comedian **Dave Attell** is host of Comedy Central's *Insomniac*.

*

Vinny Badabing is a writer and comedian from New Jersey. You can see more of his work at: www.vinnybadabing.com.

*

Comedian **Heywood Banks** has appeared on A&E's *Evening at the Improv*, MTV's *Half Hour Comedy Hour*, Showtime's Comedy Club Network, and HBO's *12th Annual Young Comedians* Special.

*

Comedian **Arj Barker** has starred in his own Comedy Central special. Website: www.arjbarker.com.

*

Comedian **Todd Barry** has appeared in his own Comedy Central special and in the movies *Road Trip* and *Pootie Tang*. Website: www.toddbarry.com.

*

Comedian **Gerry Bednob**, who likes to be known as the Turban Cowboy, is a favorite on the Vegas circuit and has been an International Star Search Champion.

*

Doug Benson is a stand-up comedian and actor whose recent television credits include NBC's *Friends* and his own Comedy Central special. Benson is also an agent provocateur of the hit off-Broadway show *The Marijuana-Logues*.

Milton Berle was a comedian who popularized TV with his early 1950s comedy show, and went on to innumerable appearances on the *Ed Sullivan* and the *Tonight Show*. Berle also starred in movies, including *It's a Mad, Mad, Mad, Mad World*.

*

Comedian **Mike Binder** has been the star and creator of the HBO series *The Mind of a Married Man*. Website: www.mikebinder.net.

*

Former Rat Pack comedian **Joey Bishop** performed in movies that ranged from *The Naked and the Dead* in 1958 to *Mad Dog Time* in 1996.

*

Comedian **Lewis Black** is a political correspondent and curmudgeon for *The Daily Show*. Website: www.lewisblack.net.

*

Comedian **Ed Bluestone** is a comedian from the 1970s who segued to book author and comedy writer known for having created the best-selling *National Lampoon* cover "Buy This Magazine or We'll Shoot This Dog."

*

Comedian **Alonzo Bodden** has been a finalist on NBC's *Last Comic Standing*. Website: www.alonzo-bodden.com.

Comedian **Joe Bolster** has performed on the *Tonight Show* with Jay Leno, in his own HBO special, and has written for both *The Martin Short Show* and the Academy Awards.

*

Comedian **Bill Braudis** has appeared on *Late Night with Conan O'Brien*, has written for Comedy Central's *Dr. Katz, Professional Therapist,* and has been the voice of Doug Savage on the animated series *Science Court.*

*

Comedian **Dylan Brody** has appeared on A&E's *Comedy on the Road* and FOX TV's *Comedy Express,* written jokes for Jay Leno's *Tonight Show* monologues, and published science fiction and fantasy novels for young adults. Website: www.dylanbrody.com.

*

Mel Brooks is a comedian, writer, and director of such films as *Young Frankenstein* and *Blazing Saddles* and the Broadway musical *The Producers.*

*

Comedian **A. Whitney Brown** has been the anchor on *Saturday Night Live's* Weekend Update, and has also been seen on Comedy Central's *The Daily Show.*

*

Comedian **Joe E. Brown's** career ranged from running away with the circus at ten to vaudeville, Broadway, and early movies, and a classic turn as millionaire Osgood Fielding III in director Billy Wilder's *Some Like It Hot.*

Comedian **Lenny Bruce** was the comedian who practically invented comedy plain-speak in the second half of the twentieth century. Bruce also produced albums that include his *Carnegie Hall Concert*, and wrote the book *How to Talk Dirty and Influence People*.

*

Comedian **Steve Bruner** has also performed on A&E's *Evening at the Improv* and Showtime's *Comedy Club Network*. Website: www.stevebruner.com.

*

Andy Bumatai is Hawaii's favorite comedian with seven albums to his credit, and appearances on TV shows that include *Baywatch*. Website: www.andybumatai.com.

*

Comedian **Red Buttons** also won the Best Supporting Actor Golden Globe and Oscar for the film *Sayonara*.

*

Godfrey Cambridge was an African American actor and comedian whose style was drawn off the racial climate of the 1950s and 1960s. One of his most memorable roles was in the 1970 film *Watermelon Man*, in which he played a white man who turned black overnight.

*

Comedian **Rob Cantrell** has been a finalist on NBC's *Last Comic Standing*.

Steve Carell is a correspondent for *The Daily Show* on Comedy Central.

*

Comedian **Drew Carey** is, coincidentally enough, the star of now-syndicated sitcom *The Drew Carey Show*.

*

Comedian **George Carlin** has won a Grammy, a CableAce award, and was nominated for an Emmy for his comedy albums and HBO and network comedy specials. Website: www.georgecarlin.com.

*

British comedian **Jimmy Carr** has performed on the English television shows *Parkinson, Never Mind the Buzzcocks* and *QI*.

*

Comedian **Jim Carrey** is the star of films that range from *Dumb and Dumber* to *The Truman Show* and *Man on the Moon*.

*

Johnny Carson hosted NBC's the *Tonight Show* for more than thirty years. Website: www.johnnycarson.com.

*

Comedian **Christopher Case** has been a writer and producer for the sitcoms *Titus* and *Reba*.

*

Comedian **Rich Ceisler** has performed on Comedy Central and HBO.

Comedian **Jeff Cesario** has won two Emmys and six CableAce awards for writing and producing *The Larry Sanders Show*, *Dennis Miller Live*, and his own HBO and Comedy Central stand-up specials. Website: www.jeffcesario.com.

*

Comedian **Vernon Chapman** has appeared in the movies *Elvis Meets Nixon* and *Billy Madison*.

*

It stands to reason that comedian **Dave Chappelle** is the host of *Chappelle's Show* on Comedy Central.

*

Comedian **Anthony Clark** is the star of the sitcom *Yes, Dear*.

*

Herb Clark is a comedian from Leeds, Alabama, who has performed on the Bacardi by Night Comedy Tour and at comedy clubs including the Comedy Zone, Summit Comedy, and Comedy House Theatre. Website: www.herbclark.com, or drop him a line at funnynobodies3@aol.com.

*

Comedian **Al Cleathen** has appeared on *Evening at the Improv* and Fox's *The Sunday Comics*.

*

Comedian **Jack Coen** has made a dozen appearances on the *Tonight Show* and, no fools, they made him a staff writer. He also recently starred in his own Comedy Central special.

Myron Cohen was a favorite comedian and story-teller on the Borscht Belt circuit and later made numerous appearances on 1950s TV, including *The Ed Sullivan Show*.

*

Comedian **Marty Cohen** has performed on *Evening at the Improv*.

*

Scotland's favorite comedian, **Billy Connolly**, has also been featured in films, including his star turn in *Her Majesty, Mrs. Brown*. Website: billyconnolly.com.

*

Comedian **Billiam Coronel** has been a staff-writer on the TV series *Men Behaving Badly* and *The Parent 'Hood*.

*

Tim Conway is a classic comedian best known for his sketch work on *The Carol Burnett Show*, and his *Dorf* videos.

*

Comedian **David Corrado** performs throughout Los Angeles, writes for several comedians and can be contacted at dcorrado@ucla.edu.

*

The title of his first comedy album was prophetic: **Bill Cosby** *Is a Very Funny Fellow, Right?* which continued to be true during a forty-year career, which includes the 1984–92 TV run of *The Cosby Show*, and his books, *Fatherhood* and *Time Flies*.

Comedian **Tom Cotter** has been featured in his own Comedy Central special.

*

Comedian **Wayne Cotter** has hosted *Comic Strip Live* on the Fox TV Network for three years. Cotter also appears regularly on *The Late Show with David Letterman* and is a roving reporter for the *Tonight Show* with Jay Leno. Website: www.waynecotter.com.

*

Comedian **Barry Crimmins** is a staff writer for *Air America Radio* and has released two CDs, *Strange Bedfellows* on A&M and *Kill the Messenger* on Green Linnet. Website: www.barrycrimmins.com.

In addition to conspiring on and creating HBO's *Mr. Show*, comedian **David Cross** has appeared in films which include *Men in Black*. Website: www.boband-david.com.

*

Comedian **Lance Crouther** originated the character Pootie Tang on the HBO's *Chris Rock Show*, and has won an Emmy and CableAce award for his writing on that show.

Comedian **Billy Crystal** is an actor in and director of movies that include *City Slickers* and *When Harry Met Sally*, and serial host of the Academy Awards.

*

Comedian **Danny Curtis's** television appearances include *America's Funniest People* on ABC. Curtis has performed at many of the nation's best comedy venues such as New York City's Dangerfield's, Atlantic City's and Las Vegas' Tropicana Hotel, the Pocono's Ceasars Hotel and the Catskill's Villa Roma. Curtis also entertains passengers on the Princess cruise line. Website: www.comedyon-theroad.com/danny_curtis.html.

*

Lee Curtis and **Jon Berahya**, two up-and-coming comedians from South Florida, are the producers of the CD "Lee & Jon, Scar Your Children for Life." Contact: LeeandJon@aol.com.

*

Comedian **Frank D'Amico** has played a recurring character on the sitcoms *Grounded For Life* and *Becker*.

*

Comedian **Rodney Dangerfield** starred in the movies *Caddyshack*, *Back to School,* and improbably enough, *Natural Born Killers*. He also won a Grammy for his comedy album *No Respect*. Website: www.rodney.com.

*

Tony Deyo is a stand-up comic from High Point, NC. Website: www.tonydeyo.com.

Comedian **Nick DiPaulo** has appeared on Comedy Central's *Comics Come Home* and *Tough Crowd with Colin Quinn.*

*

Comedian **Bob Dubac** has performed on the TV shows *Loving, Growing Pains, Life Goes On, Jack and Mike, Diff'rent Strokes,* and in his own one-man show *The Male Intellect: An Oxymoron.* Website: www.maleintellect.com.

*

Devin Dugan is a professional comedian based in Southern California, who has also published three books, including *Texas Midnight.* Website: www.devindugan.com.

*

Comedian **Mike Dugan** has appeared on the *Tonight Show with Jay Leno,* and won an Emmy Award for writing on HBO's *Dennis Miller: Live.* Dugan is also the author of the one-man show *Men Fake Foreplay.* Website: www.menfakeforeplay.com.

*

Political comedian **Will Durst** was host of the award-winning PBS series *We Do the Work,* taped a *One Night Stand* for HBO, and starred in A&E's *A Year's Worth with Will Durst,* which was nominated for a CableAce Award. Durst also has been nominated five times for an American Comedy Award but still hasn't won, making him the Susan Lucci of stand-up. Website: www.willdurst.com.

Dwight is a Los Angeles-based actor and comedian.

*

Comedian **Bil Dwyer** has appeared on most of the defunct stand-up shows, and has had guest-starring roles on *The Larry Sanders Show* and *Ally McBeal*.

*

Comedian **Dana Eagle** has performed at the Aspen Comedy Festival, on Showtime and the Oxygen Network, in Comedy Central's *Premium Blend*, and in a bunch of commercials. Contact: dana@laughter-heals.org.

*

Comedian **Chas Elstner** has performed at hundreds of comedy clubs including Comic Strip Live. He has also performed as an opening act for Gloria Estefan, and appeared on MTV and Showtime.

*

Comedian **Bill Engvall** has won an American Comedy Award and is a star of Comedy Central's *Blue Collar Comedy*. Website: www.billengvall.com.

*

Comedian **Bob Ettinger** has appeared on *Evening at the Improv* and Showtime's *Comedy Club Network*.

*

Comedian **Wayne Federman** has been featured in his own Comedy Central special, on HBO's *Curb Your Enthusiasm*, and in the movie *50 First Dates*.

Jimmy Fallon has been a *Saturday Night Live* cast member and co-host of *Weekend Update*.

*

Michael Feldman has been featured in the book *That's Funny*.

*

A father of five, **Ken Ferguson** performs comedy in the Midwest. "I need to tell the world how ticked off I am, and make people laugh at the same time." Contact: Kenfergy2@aol.com.

*

Comedian **Adam Ferrara** has been featured on the ABC sitcom *The Job*, and has been twice nominated for an American Comedy Award. Website: www.adamferrara.com.

*

Comedian **Jeff Foxworthy** is the star of Comedy Central's *Blue Collar Comedy*.

*

Redd Foxx was a stand-up comedian for over forty years and the star of the 1970s sitcom *Sanford and Son*.

*

Comedian **Zach Galifianakis** has been a star of the TV show *Tru Calling* and a writer for *That '70s Show*.

*

Gallagher is the giant-prop and watermelon-smashing comedian whose Showtime specials are frequently aired on Comedy Central. Website: www.gallaghers-mash.com.

Comedian **Billy Garan** has appeared on Showtime, Comedy Central, and in films including *Indecent Proposal*.

*

Larry Getlen is a New York-based comedian, journalist, and actor who has written for *Esquire* magazine and Comedy Central's *Tough Crowd with Colin Quinn*, and appeared on *Chappelle's Show*. Website: zhet.blogspot.com.

*

Irv Gilman is a comedian, MC, and former Council Member of Monterey Park, California.

*

In addition to being a finalist on NBC's *Last Comic Standing*, comedian **Todd Glass** has appeared on numerous other TV shows, including *Home Improvement*, *Friends*, *Married with Children* and HBO's *Mr. Show*. Website: www.toddglass.com.

*

Comedian **Bob Goldthwait** has starred in the movie *Scrooged* and on TV series that include *Unhappily Ever After*. Bob has also directed the movie *Shakes the Clown*, and *Chapelle's Show* on Comedy Central.

*

Reno Goodale is a comedian, writer and actor who has written material for Roseanne and Jay Leno, and performed as the opening act for Joan Rivers and Dana Carvey. Goodale has appeared in national commercials and on network television, and also headlines in clubs and colleges across the country.

Mark Guido is a San Francisco-based comedian.

*

Comedian **Gary Gulman** has been a finalist on NBC's *Last Comic Standing*. Website: www.garygulman.com.

*

Comedian **Geechy Guy** has appeared on the *Tonight Show*, MTV, and Comedy Central. Website: www.geechyguy.com.

*

Comedian **Doug Graham** has performed as an openign act for many national acts including Drew Carey, Kevin Meaney, Phoebe Snow, and Spyrogyra.

*

Dick Gregory is a groundbreaking African-American political comedian and civil rights activist, still active in both. Website: www.dickgregory.com.

*

Ex-Bostonian **Adam Gropman** is a Los Angeles-based stand-up comic, writer and actor who contributes to sheckymagazine.com and hollywoodbadass.com.

*

Comedian **Arsenio Hall** has been the host of *Star Search* and *The Arsenio Hall Show*.

*

Deric Harrington is a comedian who likes his web site, www.dericharrington.com. He also likes the taste of victory.

Comedian **Alan Havey** has hosted *Night after Night* on the nascent Comedy Channel and appeared in the movies *Internal Affairs, Rounders,* and *Wild Things2.* Website: www.allanhavey.com.

*

Comedian **Mitch Hedberg** has performed on *That '70s Show* and in his own stand-up special on Comedy Central. Website: www.mitchhedberg.net.

*

John Heffron has been the winning comedian and last comic standing on NBC's *Last Comic Standing.* Website: www.johnheffron.com.

*

Kevin Hench, TV producer and comedy writer, is supervising producer of *The Sports List* on Fox Sports Net.

*

In the 1980s and early 1990s comedian **Bill Hicks** made eleven appearances on the David Letterman show, and released his first concert video, *Sane Man.* Hicks recorded four comedy albums during his lifetime (including *Dangerous* and *Relentless*), and the albums *Arizona Bay* and *Rant in E-Minor,* which were issued posthumously. Website: www.billhicks.com.

*

British comic **Benny Hill** was best known in America for his slapstick syndicated TV show *The Benny Hill Show.*

Comedian **Steve Hofstetter** is the author of the *Student Body Shots* series, available in bookstores everywhere. Website: www.stevehofstetter.com.

*

Comedian **Corey Holcomb** has been a finalist on the second season of NBC's *Last Comic Standing*.

*

Bob Hope was a comedian whose career ranged over seven decades from vaudeville to a series of *Road* movies with Bing Crosby and innumerable television specials.

*

Comedian **D.L. Hughley** has been the star of the sitcom *The Hughleys*, and has appeared in the films *Inspector Gadget* and *Scary Movie*.

*

Comedian **Dom Irrera** has starred in his own HBO specials and also appeared on TV shows that include *Everybody Loves Raymond* and *The Drew Carey Show* and movies that include *The Big Lebowski*.

*

Comedian **Jeff Jena** has been seen on over forty national television shows, and currently owns a comedy club in Newport, Kentucky. Contact: JeffreyTJ@aol.com.

*

Comedian **Richard Jeni** has been rewarded for his comic fluidity with two CableAce Awards and one American Comedy Award. Website: www.richard-jeni.com.

Comedian **Jake Johannsen** has starred in his own HBO One Night Stand, and was nominated for an American Comedy Award. Website: www.jakethis.com.

*

Comedian **Norman K**. performs at clubs in the New York area. Contact: normank_comic@hotmail.com.

*

Comedian **Bill Kalmenson** has appeared in the movie *Lethal Weapon* and has been the screenwriter and director of the film *The Souler Opposite*.

*

Stand-up comedian and actor **Gabe Kaplan** is best known for playing the title role in the 1970s television series *Welcome Back Kotter*.

*

Myq Kaplan performs music and comedy in the Boston area, is a regular at the Comedy Studio, and an irregular elsewhere. His CD is titled "Open Myq Night." Website: www.myqkaplan.com

*

Comedian **Jonathan Katz** has played doctor on Comedy Central's *Dr. Katz, Professional Therapist* and is the author of *To Do Lists of the Dead*.

*

Comedian **Patrick Keane** has appeared at the Irvine Improv, the Comedy Store, Mixed Nuts, the Ha Ha Café, and other comedy venues throughout Southern California.

Comedian **Bobby Kelton** has appeared on *The Tonight Show* and the *Late Show with David Letterman*.

*

Former Canadian fighter pilot and now comedian **Barry Kennedy** has appeared on A&E's *Comedy on the Road*. He is also the author of two books.

*

Comedian **Brian Kiley** is an Emmy-nominated writer who appears regularly on the *Tonight Show* and *Late Night with Conan O'Brien*.

*

Comedian **Craig Kilborn** has been the host of CBS's *The Late Late Show*.

*

Comedian **Nosmo King** is co-creator of the Los Angeles showcase "Dreamland."

*

Comedian **Mark Klein** has performed on A&E's *Comedy on the Road* and Showtime's *Comedy Club Network*. Website: www.corpjester.com.

*

Comedian **Tommy Koenig** has been a mainstay on the national comedy scene since the early 1980s and founded The Comics Studio in 1999 in New York to help a new generation of comics. Website: www.comicsstudio.com.

Political comedian **Paul Krassner's** CD *We Have Ways of Making You Laugh* has been released by Mercury Records.

*

Comedian **Bob Kubota** has appeared on *Evening at the Improv*, MTV *Half Hour Comedy Hour,* and *Entertainment Tonight.*

*

Comedian **Rocky LaPorte** has performed on *Comic Strip Live*, A&E's *Evening at the Improv,* and Caroline's *Comedy Hour.*

*

Comedian **Todd Larson** performs regularly at the Rivercenter Comedy Club, and has worked with such talented comedians as Chris Fonseca and Shawn Gnandt. Contact: acelarson@aol.com.

*

Comedian **Denis Leary** stars in the FX Network series *Rescue Me*, his own HBO specials, and a number of films including *The Ref* and *Two if By Sea.*

*

Comedian **James Leemer** has appeared on Comedy Central's *Dr. Katz Professional Therapist.*

*

David Letterman is the host of CBS's *Late Show.*

Danny Liebert is a best-selling bumper sticker writer ("Jesus is Coming — Look Busy") who has segued into performing comedy at the Comic Strip, Stand-up NY, Caroline's, and numerous more ephemeral venues. Contact: dliebert@msn.com.

*

Comedian **Jay Leno** is host of NBC's *The Tonight Show*.

*

In addition to his numerous HBO specials, comedian **Richard Lewis** has starred in the sitcom *Anything But Love*, and in the Mel Brooks movie *Robin Hood: Men in Tights*. Website: richardlewisonline.com.

*

Comedian **Jay London** has been a finalist on NBC's *Last Comic Standing*.

*

Comedian **George Lopez** is the star of the *George Lopez* show on ABC. Website: www.georgelopez.com.

*

Jason Love is a comedian whose cartoon *Snapshots* has garnered a worldwide audience through syndication in 32 newspapers, dozens of magazines, 500 websites, and a line of greeting cards. Website: www.jasonlove.com.

*

Comedian **Al Lubel** has performed on *Evening at the Improv* and *Comic Strip Live* and has been a featured patient on Comedy Central's *Dr. Katz*.

Mark Lundholm has taken his "twelve-step comedy" to comedy clubs and detox centers across country. Website: www.marklundholm.com.

*

Daniel Lybra is a Roundtable Comedy Conference award-winning comedian and comedy writer.

*

Comedian **Bernie Mac** has performed on TV's *Bernie Mac* Show and in movies including *Ocean's 11* and *Bad Santa*.

*

Comedian **Mike MacDonald** has starred in three Showtime and CBS specials including "*Mike MacDonald: On Target.*"

*

Comedian **Norm Macdonald** has showcased his wry smirk as a stand-up anchor on *Saturday Night Live*, followed by the eponymous smirk sitcom *Norm*, and movies such as *Dirty Laundry*.

*

Comedian **Erik Mackenroth** has been a finalist in Orange County's Funniest Person Contest, and appeared on the TV show *Extreme Gong*. Website: www.ErikMackenroth.com.

*

Comedian **Dexter Madison** has appeared on the TV shows *Evening at the Improv* and PBS's *Comedy Tonight*.

Comedian **Bill Maher** is the host of HBO's *Real Time with Bill Maher*. Who'd a thunk it?

*

Comedian **Howie Mandel** has been the star of the series *St. Elsewhere*, the creator of his own animated series *Bobby's World*, and the host of *The Howie Mandel Show*. Website: www.howiemandel.com.

*

Jackie Mason has been a forty-year comedy veteran and the star of several one-man Broadway shows. Website: www.jackiemason.com.

*

Comedian **Demetri Martin** tells jokes in New York City. Website: www.demetrimartin.com.

*

Steve Martin is a comedian who starred in, wrote, and directed comedy films including *The Jerk* and *Bowfinger*.

*

Groucho Marx was a comedian who, with The Marx Brothers, made a number of the funniest films of the 1930s, including *Duck Soup*, and whose marvelous 1950s game show *You Bet Your Life*, still deserves viewing on some cable channel smart enough to feature it.

*

Comedian **Dobie Maxwell** has had an amazing life. His parents were bikers, and his best friend from childhood robbed a bank *twice*, and tried to blame the second robbery on Dobie. Despite that, Dobie has survived to become a morning radio host and comedian who headlines across the USA. Website: www.dobiemaxwell.com.

*

John McGivern is an actor, writer and comedian who has appeared on the HBO's *We're Funny That Way*, and Comedy Central's *Out There II*. Website: www.johnmcgivern.com.

*

Comedian **John Mendoza** has appeared on the *Tonight Show* and was one of Showtime's *Pair of Jokers*.

*

Comedian **Dennis Miller** is the possessor of God-given sarcasm and the star of CNBC's *Dennis Miller*.

*

During a three-decade comedy career, comedian **George Miller** was a frequent guest on national television talk shows, including *Late Night with David Letterman*.

*

British comedian **Spike Milligan** is the favorite comic of Prince Charles and, when presented a British Comedy award for Lifetime Achievement, Spike famously rewarded the prince by calling Charles "a groveling little bastard" on live TV.

*

Gene Mitchener is a motivational speaker and self-proclaimed America's Funniest Sit-Down Comic.

Improv comedian **Colin Mocherie** is one of the inventive stars of *Whose Line is it Anyway?*

*

In his twenty-five year career as a comedian **Kelly Monteith** has starred in his own BBC television series and appeared on numerous American television shows, including the *Tonight Show* and Comedy Central's *The Daily Show.*

*

Comedian **Steve Moris** has performed as the opening act for the Beach Boys since the 1980s. Moris also has opened in Las Vegas for comic great Louie Anderson, and travels the world headlining comedy shows for Celebrity Cruise Lines. Website: www.stevemoris.com.

*

Gary Muledeer has had a 30-year comedy career that includes over 250 TV appearances.

*

Steve Neal is a Los Angeles-based comedian and the writer of his critically-acclaimed, one-man show "The Great White Trash Hope." Website: www.steve-neal.net.

*

Kevin Nealon is a headlining comedian, actor, and one of the longest-running cast members on *Saturday Night Live.*

Comedian **Taylor Negron** has performed on TV shows which include *Friends* and *Seinfeld* and movies such as *Stuart Little* and *Angels in the Outfield*.

*

Buzz Nutley is a professional comedian who has written for the *Pittsburgh Post Gazette* and *Los Angeles Times*, has sold material to Jay Leno and Yakov Smirnoff, and has performed as the opening act for Jon Stewart. Website: www.buzznutley.com.

*

Conan O'Brien, a former writer for *Saturday Night Live* and *The Simpsons*, is the host of the NBC talk show, *Late Night with Conan O'Brien*.

*

Irish comedian **Owen O'Neill** has performed at the Montreal Comedy Festival, and has been a guest on *Late Night with Conan O'Brien*.

*

Rob O'Reilly is a Cleveland comedian who has played venues which include the Cleveland Improv and the Comedy Connections. Contact: rob84@bu.edu.

*

P.J. O'Rourke is a humorist, satirist, and the author of several books including *Modern Manners* and *Eat the Rich*.

*

Comedian **Patton Oswalt** has appeared on the sitcom *Seinfeld*, and is a cast member of CBS's *King of Queens*. Website: www.pattonoswalt.com.

Comedian **Pat Paulsen** was featured on the groundbreaking *Smothers Brothers Show*, and satirically ran for president for three decades.

Dave Pavone is a stand-up comedian and comedy writer based in Phoenix, Arizona. He is the co-creator of "The Timmy Sketch Project" a local comedy sketch show. Contact: dbpavone@yahoo.com.

*

Comedian **Jackson Perdue** is a casino favorite in Las Vegas and Tahoe, and has also appeared on the Playboy Channel.

*

Gene Perret has written comedy material for over 30 years for legends such as Phyllis Diller, Bob Hope, Carol Burnett and Bill Cosby. Perret has won three Emmys and a Writers Guild Award for his TV comedy writing, and has published 25 books on humor, including *Comedy Writing Step by Step*. Website: http://www.members.aol.com/geneperret/.

*

Comedian **Emo Philips** has appeared on numerous HBO and Showtime specials, as well as in the "Weird" Al Yankovich movie *UHF*. Website: www.emophilips.com.

*

In addition to having been one of the frightfully inventive stars of Comedy Central's *Whose Line is it Anyway*, comedian **Greg Proops** has been the host of their game shows *Vs* and *Rendez-View*. Website: www.gregproops.com.

Comedian **Paul Provenza** has starred on the last season of *Northern Exposure*, and in his own HBO, Showtime, and Comedy Central shows and series.

*

Comedian **Richard Pryor** is a nearly forty-year veteran of comedy recording, movies, and TV, including the ground-breaking 1970s *Richard Pryor Show*, and the movie *Silver Streak*. Website: www.richardpryor.com.

*

Comedian **Greg Ray** has been seen on *Evening at the Improv*, CNN and PM Magazine. But he is perhaps best known for holding the watermelon in the Ginsu knife commercials.

*

Comedian **Larry Reeb** has appeared on Showtime's *Comedy Club All-Stars*, and A&E's *Evening at the Improv*.

*

Comedian **Alex Reed** has performed on *Evening at the Improv*.

*

Comedian **Brian Regan** has appeared on the *Tonight Show with Jay Leno* and in his own Comedy Central and Showtime specials. Website: www.brianregan.com.

*

Comedian **Paul Reiser** is the star and creator of the now-syndicated sitcom based on his marriage, *Mad About You*.

Comedian **Ron Richards** won an Emmy Award for his writing on *Late Night with David Letterman*, and a CableAce Award for HBO's *Not Necessarily the News*. Richards has also been on the writing staff of the *Tonight Show*, and NBC's *Saturday Night Live*.

*

Comedian **Adam Richmond** has appeared on Nickelodeon, Fox Sports Net, and in several national commercials. He has been a staff writer for the Canadian animated series *Chilly Beach*. Contact: gunnyfuy@yahoo.com.

*

Johnny Robish is a comedian whose jokes appear frequently in the Laugh Lines column of the *Los Angeles Times*, and whose gigglebytes are featured in the Internet radio program *Radio Free OZ*.

*

Mo Rocca is a former correspondent for Comedy Central's *The Daily Show*, a contributor to NBC's *Today Show*, and the host of Bravo's *Things I Hate About You*.

*

Comedian **Paul Rodriguez** has been the star of the first Hispanic sitcom on network TV, *AKA Pablo,* in the 1970s and has also starred in the movies *Born in East LA, Made in America,* and *Rough Magic.*

*

Comedian **Kenny Rogerson** has appeared on Comedy Central, MTV, and Showtime and in the movie *There's Something About Mary.*

Comedian **Ray Romano** is the star of the CBS series *Everybody Loves Raymond*, and the author of the best-selling book *Everything, and a Kite*.

*

Comedian **John Ross** has also appeared on TV shows which include *Coach* and *St. Elsewhere*.

*

Philadelphia comedian **Eric Roth** won "Philly's Last Local Comic Standing" contest. Contact: Emroth@aol.com.

*

Comedian **Jeffrey Ross** has both written for, and performed on, Comedy Central.

*

Comedian **Mike Rowe** has been featured on NBC's *Comedy Showcase*, and was a featured patient on Comedy Central's *Dr. Katz, Professional Therapist*.

*

Bob Rubin is a San Francisco-based comedian and author of the play *I Never Knew My Father*.

*

Comedian **Mike Rubin** has been a writer on Comedy Central's *Crank Yankers*, and a producer of *The Bachelor*. Contact: michaeldiehard@yahoo.com.

Comedian **Tom Ryan's** national television appearances include performances on *Late Show with David Letterman*, Showtime, A&E, and Comedy Central. He has also performed as an opening act for

B. B. King, Tim Allen and Steven Wright. Website: www.comediantomryan.com.

*

Comedian **Dan St. Paul** has appeared on *An Evening at the Improv* and VH-1's *Stand-Up Spotlight* and in the movie *Flubber*.

*

Jim Samuels was a beloved San Francisco-based comedian who died in 1990.

*

Comedian **Adam Sandler** is a former cast member of NBC's *Saturday Night Live* and the star of a string of comedy movies, including *Happy Gilmore*, *The Waterboy*, and The *Wedding Singer*. Website: www.adamsandler.com.

*

Comedian **Peter Sasso** performs in comedy clubs and on cruise ships. Contact: sassopeter@hotmail.com.

*

Comedian **Drake Sather** wrote for numerous TV shows, including *News Radio*, *The Dennis Miller Show*, and *Ed*, received an Emmy nomination for his work on *The Larry Sanders Show*, and co-wrote the movie *Zoolander* with actor Ben Stiller.

*

Comedian **Robert Schimmel** has been featured in his own HBO Special and his CDs include, *If You Buy This CD, I Can Buy This Car*, *Robert Schimmel Comes Clean*, and *Unprotected*. Website: robertschimmel.com.

Comedian **Jerry Seinfeld** helped rethink the sitcom with his eponymous *Seinfeld*.

*

Six-time Emmy Award winning comedian **Ross Shafer** was a host of *Match Game*, and the *Miss America Pageant*.

Ronnie Shakes was a comedian and TV writer who made frequent appearances on *The Tonight Show*.

*

Comedian **Garry Shandling** is the star and creator of *The Larry Sanders Show* and frequent host of the Emmy Awards show.

*

Comedian **Shang** has costarred on *The Jamie Foxx Show* and has been featured in the Best of the Fest on the HBO's *U.S. Comedy Arts Festival* special. Website: www.iamshang.com.

Craig Sharf is a comedian and comedy writer who has sold material to professional comedians, including Joan Rivers, and to other comedy outlets such as the *Weinerville* TV show. Contact: csharf@yahoo.com.

Jeff Shaw is a comedian, humor columnist, and staff writer in the Alternative Cards department of Cleveland's American Greetings Corporation. Contact: Dork2Dude@aol.com.

*

Comedian **Craig Shoemaker** has appeared on over 100 television shows including HBO's *Comic Relief* and *Hollywood Squares* and his film appearances include *Scream2* and *The Lovemaster*. Website: www.craigshoemaker.com.

*

Comedian and actor **Thom Sharp's** bald-faced mug is a TV commercial staple for such products as Goodyear tires and General Electric refrigerators.

*

Comedian **Will Shriner** has also directed episodes of *Everybody Loves Raymond*, and won a Humanitas Award for his direction of an episode of *Frasier*.

*

Comedian **Jimmy Shubert** was featured at the Just for Laughs Montreal Comedy Festival and in the movies *GO*, *Coyoye Ugly,* and *The Italian Job*. Website: jimmyshubert.com.

*

Comedian **Ritch Shydner** has written for the sitcom *Roseanne*, and appeared on the TV shows *Married with Children*, and *Designing Women*. He has also starred in feature films, such as *Beverly Hills Cop II* and *Roxanne*.

Comedian **Sinbad** has starred in several of his own HBO specials including *Son of a Preacher Man*, and in a number of movies, including *House Guest* and *First Kid*.

*

Comedian **Steve Skrovan** has written for the sitcom *Seinfeld*.

*

Comedian **Brad Slaight** has segued from the recurring role of Izzy Adams on *The Young and the Restless* to stand-up comedy and contributing writer to the *Tonight Show*. Website: http://members.aol.com/bisbprods/.

*

Comedian **Bobby Slayton** has appeared in the movies *Ed Wood*, *Get Shorty*, *Bandits*, and also portrayed Joey Bishop in the HBO movie *The Rat Pack*. Website: www.bobbyslayton.com.

*

Comedian **Tommy Sledge**, "Stand-up Detective," has appeared on Showtime, TNN and HBO. Website: www.comedypro.com/sledge/.

Comedian **Bruce Smirnoff's** award-winning one-man show is titled *Other Than My Health, I Have Nothing...And Today I Don't Feel So Good*.

*

Bob Smith, one of the first openly gay comics on TV and the *Tonight Show*, is also the author of the book *Openly Bob*. Website: http://literati.net/Smith/.

Canadian comedian **Steve Smith** is also a writer, producer, and past recipient of the Banff Television Festival's Sir Peter Ustinov Comedy Network Award.

*

Dana Snow has been doing stand-up for centuries and has written for comedians, including Phyllis Diller. Two of his movie scripts have been optioned, including one based on a joke he wrote for Billy Crystal for the 1997 Academy Awards. Contact: supersnow@hotmail.com.

*

Spanky has been voted "1999 Comedian of the Year" by the Campus Activities Reader's Choice Awards. Also, in 1999, Spanky made his 35th television appearance on PBS's *Comics A to Z*.

*

Comedian **Tim Steeves** has been featured at the Just for Laughs Montreal Comedy Festival.

*

Comedian **Skip Stephenson** was also one of the hosts of the 1980s TV show *Real People*.

*

Comedian **Jon Stewart** is the host of Comedy Central's *The Daily Show*.

*

Comedian **Fred Stoller** has written for the sitcom *Seinfeld*, has appeared on the TV shows *Everybody Loves Raymond* and *Six Feet Under*, and in the movies *Austin Powers* and *Dumb and Dumber*.

Strange de Jim has been San Francisco's leading town-fool since 1972, and is author of a photo history of San Francisco's Castro district. Website: www.members.aol.com/mrdejim/.

*

Comedian **Glenn Super** appeared on the TV shows *Evening at the Improv*, *Comic Strip Live*, and *Solid Gold*, but Dr. Demento's radio fans may remember him best through his novelty number "Good Sex" (*The Dr. Ruth Song*).

*

Dave Thomas is a graduate of the legendary *SCTV* and has since been seen all over the dial from *Grace under Fire* to *That '70s Show*.

*

Comedian **Paul F. Tompkins** has won an Emmy as a writer for HBO's *Mr. Show*, and also appeared on *Real Time with Bill Maher*. Website: www.paulftompkins.com.

*

Comedian **Greg Travis** is also an actor who has appeared on the TV shows *CSI: Miami* and *JAG* and in the movies *Man on the Moon* and *Starship Troopers*.

*

Comedian **Jeff Valdez** is the cofounder and chairman of cable network Sí TV, and was the creator of Nickelodeon's *Brothers Garcia*.

Matt Vance has been the morning show producer for *Mick & Allen's Freak Show* on Rock 99 radio Salt Lake City.

*

King of the deadpan comics, **Jackie Vernon** made frequent appearances on the *Ed Sullivan Show*. His wry, sad-sack style influenced some of today's most popular comedians.

*

Comedian **Charlie Viracola** has had his own two half-hour specials on both Showtime and Comedy Central. Website: www.planetcharlie.com.

*

Comedian **Rich Voss** has been a finalist on NBC's *Last Comic Standing*. Website: www.richvos.com.

*

John Wagner is the creator of the alternative comic *Judge Dredd*.

*

Comedian **George Wallace** is a regular performer on both the *Tonight Show* and *Late Night with David Letterman*.

*

Wally Wang is a comedian and an actor who, in his latest performance on the Internet, managed to convince thousands of men that he's actually a 23-year-old blonde. Wang also has appeared on A&E's *Evening at the Improv*, performs in Las Vegas, wrote the books *Visual Basic for Dummies*, *Microsoft Office*

For Dummies, and publishes a computer humor column in *Boardwatch Magazine*.

*

Joel Warshaw has performed for his family and friends for years, and can now also be seen performing in Los Angeles at the Comedy Store and at the LA Cabaret Comedy Club.

*

Comedian **Damon Wayans** has been the star and one of the creators of *In Living Color*, and has starred in several movies including *The Last Boy Scout*, and three of his own HBO specials.

*

Comedian **Matt Weinhold** won the Seattle Comedy Competition and has appeared on Showtime, MTV, and Comedy Central.

*

Comedian **Basil White** is a weird, scary man-child. Know all at: www.basilwhite.com.

*

Slappy White was a classic comedian whose career ranged from the Catskills to the *Ed Sullivan Show*.

Comedian **Dan Whitney's** Larry the Cable Guy is featured on nearly 200 radio stations nationwide, and has also been seen on Comedy Central's *Blue Collar Comedy*.

Comedian **Harland Williams** has hosted Comedy Central's *Premium Blend* and appeared in films which include *The Whole Nine Yards* and *Half-Baked*. Website: www.harlandwilliams.com.

*

Comedian **Robin Williams** received an Academy Award for *Good Will Hunting* and is the star of dozens of other movies including *Mrs. Doubtfire* and *Flubber*.

*

Comedian **Eric S. Wilson** has appeared on the *Tonight Show with Jay Leno*.

*

Comedian **Jonathan Winters** is an Emmy Award winner and has been nominated for 12 Grammy Awards. Website: www.jonathanwinters.com.

*

Comedian **Woody Woodbury** has been featured in the movie *For Those Who Think Young* and his early 1960s comedy albums include *Laughing Room* and *Saloonatics*.

*

Comedian **Fred Wolf** is the screenwriter responsible for the movies *Black Sheep* and *Joe Dirt*.

*

Comedian **Robert Wuhl** has been the protagonist and creator of HBO's sitcom *Arli$$*.

Steven Wright has appeared on numerous HBO specials, was a recurring cast member of the sitcom *Mad about You,* and has received an Oscar nomination for Best Short Film. Website: www.stevenwright.com.

*

Jim Wyatt is a stand-up comedian, and animation producer of *Garfield* and *The Twisted Tales of Felix the Cat.*

*

Weird Al Yankovic's CD of comedy songs, *Poodle Hat,* has won a Grammy for Best Comedy Album of 2003. This is Al's third Grammy win, including Best Comedy Recording in 1984 for *Eat It* and Best Concept Video in 1988 for *Fat.* Website: www.weirdal.com.

*

Henny Youngman was a self-proclaimed "king of the one-liners" whose comedy career ranged from vaudeville and the Catskills to Johnny Carson's *Tonight Show.*

*

Comedian **Bob Zany** has appeared on *The Drew Carey Show, The Tonight Show,* and in films which include *Joe Dirt.*

*

Comedian and philosopher **David Zasloff** is also a musician with two CDs to his credit, including *Born to be Happy.* website: www.davidzasloff.com.